M000187328

Praise for *Messy Church Goes Wild*

'Nature is bursting with inspiration. No wonder Jesus encouraged his followers to take a good look at the birds and the flowers. The creator's fingerprints are in open view when we step outside. Here is a resource that brings together the enthusiasm and freshness of Messy Church with the wonder and awe of the great outdoors. Coming at a time when many of us are rediscovering our deep connection with nature and eager to escape domesticated forms of church, it is timely and hugely stimulating.'

Steve Aisthorpe, mission development worker for the Church of Scotland

'The environmental crisis is deepening. Many people love being outdoors, particularly children. Outdoor worship has become more and more popular. Messy Church is a rapidly growing worldwide movement. Put those facts together, and you can see why we need this book! The book begins with simple guides to the issues, and gives us some ideas on what the Bible has to say about it all. There are then case studies from around the world, and some ideas for Messy Church Goes Wild sessions. So if your Messy Church is wanting to do stuff outdoors, this will be a great place to start. But if you are not (yet!) running a Messy Church, there is also a lot in here to inspire you in outdoor worship. A great resource.'

Dr Martin J. Hodson, operations director, The John Ray Initiative

15 The Chambers, Vineyard
Abingdon OX14 3FE
brf.org.uk

Bible Reading Fellowship is a charity (233280)
and company limited by guarantee (301324),
registered in England and Wales

ISBN 978 1 80039 009 6
First published 2022
10 9 8 7 6 5 4 3 2 1 0
All rights reserved

Text © individual authors 2022
This edition © Bible Reading Fellowship 2022
Cover images © Jocelyn Czerwonka; © Nelleke Plomp at Kliederkerk
Inside images © individual authors; pp. 15, 81 © Jean Pienaar,
p. 125 © Nelleke Plomp

The authors assert the moral right to be identified as the authors of this work

Acknowledgements
Unless otherwise acknowledged, scripture quotations are taken from The Holy
Bible, New International Version (Anglicised edition) copyright © 1979, 1984, 2011
by Biblica. Used by permission of Hodder & Stoughton Publishers, a Hachette
UK company. All rights reserved. 'NIV' is a registered trademark of Biblica. UK
trademark number 1448790.

Scripture quotations marked KJV are taken from The Authorised Version of the
Bible (The King James Bible), the rights in which are vested in the Crown, are
reproduced by permission of the Crown's Patentee, Cambridge University Press.

Scripture quotations marked NRSV are taken from The New Revised Standard
Version of the Bible, Anglicised edition, copyright © 1989, 1995 by the Division of
Christian Education of the National Council of the Churches of Christ in the United
States of America. Used by permission. All rights reserved.

Scripture quotations marked MSG are taken from *The Message*, copyright © 1993,
1994, 1995, 1996, 2000, 2001, 2002 by Eugene H. Peterson. Used by permission of
NavPress. All rights reserved. Represented by Tyndale House Publishers, Inc.

Every effort has been made to trace and contact copyright owners for
material used in this resource. We apologise for any inadvertent omissions
or errors, and would ask those concerned to contact us so that full
acknowledgement can be made in the future.

A catalogue record for this book is available from the British Library

Printed with vegetable-oil based inks by Gutenberg Press, Tarxien, Malta

FSC
www.fsc.org
MIX
Paper from
responsible sources
FSC® C022612

Caring for the world we live in

Edited by **Lucy Moore**

This book is dedicated with much love and gratitude to the inspirational Jane Leadbetter who, during her time on the BRF Messy Church team, galvanised our thinking about our Messy responsibilities to God's planet. The generous gifts from the Messy Church community around the world to mark Jane's retirement in December 2020 have helped cover the extra costs of making this physical book as environmentally friendly as possible.

Contents

PART II: MESSY RESPONSES

PART III: SESSION OUTLINES

Introduction

Lucy Moore

 Lucy Moore is the founder of Messy Church. She is the author of a number of books for BRF and is now head of the Growing Faith Foundation for the Church of England. She is on the team of her local Messy Church.

What's it about, this Messy Church Goes Wild? Is the Messy Church team suddenly expert in the great outdoors? No, emphatically not. But sometimes you feel the tidal pull in your ministry drawing you in a particular direction and you can't ignore the compulsion to follow and see where it all takes you. In about 2017–18, that was the sense we had as a team. We'd been aware for many years that one of the ways children in particular find it easy to meet with God, to sense the numinous, to tap into something full of awe and wonder, to wander into the thin places of the world, is out in nature. If it is true of children, it may also be true of many adults. Church buildings for some are places that make it easier to worship; for others they can be oppressive. Perhaps we were sensing something about going out to another 'edge' and finding a new group of people who have an affinity with meeting God through the glory of the natural world.

One team member, Jane Leadbetter, to whom this book is dedicated with much affection, felt herself propelled into doing whatever she could to combat the wastage and pollution caused by single-use plastics. This led the team into a growing awareness of environmental issues. Jane's chapter explains more about her passion for marine life and her fury about plastic waste.

Messy Church has always been humbly rooted in practicalities, and another aspect of this environmental concern was our responsibility as a network in worshipping through a very 'stuff-hungry' format. In other words, you need a great deal of equipment and materials to put on a Messy Church. What could we do to encourage leaders to use natural materials instead of synthetic ones, to recycle and upcycle instead of buying more and still more new products, to take seriously our responsibilities towards the planet with regard to what we cook for the meal, what we use to eat and drink from and how we handle food waste? It's interesting that when one of the Scandinavian Messy Churches was invited to write a case study for this book about how they do Messy Church sustainably in their country, they refused, on the grounds that it was so obvious that care for the environment was a given, they couldn't possibly write anything meaningful. Worldwide, it would be great if every country were at this point in our ecological awareness, but sadly many countries have a long way to go. At the very least we can start reading, thinking and talking together about it. Hence this book!

Another tidal tug towards the outdoors being somewhere to explore was lockdown, of course. During the pandemic, plenty of Messy Churches in the UK looked seriously at the outdoors as a safer place to meet, rather than second-best to a building. Messy Church trails took place; churchyards, church gardens and parks saw Messy picnics; and Messy Church in a box, bag or even bucket were distributed. Other countries have been meeting outdoors for far longer, not having the joyous unpredictability of the British weather to contend with.

Lastly, perhaps it's worth mentioning the tradition in Messy Church of not relying on words as the sole means of communication, but instead trying to move away from the printed word, lengthy liturgies, scripture pinned down to paper and ink. Allowing the activities themselves to communicate the truths of scripture has always been important, non-verbal communication being as important as (perhaps more important than) verbal communication. This helps as we venture outside. When you're miserably aware that your favourite Bible or your carefully printed handouts are going to be reduced to papier mâché by a downpour, or blown away to litter the countryside in a gale, you look for other means of communicating, other ways of praying, of singing, of storytelling, rather than depending on the printed word.

Our family moved from Hampshire to the Peak District between lockdowns. From our new, very rural location (our nearest neighbours are sheep), let me mention three things which illustrate something of why I think God is drawing Messy Church into a fresh sense of concern for the planet: a pond, a walled garden and an Easter morning.

I am ridiculously proud of my wildlife pond. What better thing to do during lockdown in a new garden but to dig out a pond? I read up on the need for shallow pebbly beaches, indigenous plant life and the ever-present threat of blanket weed. I had yearnings for great crested newts and envisaged them stampeding in their hundreds up the hill to immerse themselves in my amphibian luxury spa. What I got was a rat. And the world's laziest pigeon, which more or less falls off the drystone wall into the pond when it wants a drink or a bath. And an obese squirrel, which frankly could use some exercise legging it down to the stream for a drink, rather than chilling out by my pond. As well as these less-welcome guests, to be fair, my malevolent diving beetles are huge fun, the pond skaters and hoverflies keep things lively and a growing colony of great pond snails have appeared from nowhere and evidently find it a romantic spot, as they grow in number daily.

Why did I feel the urge to build a pond? Because human beings have used up so much of the countryside for building, altering the watery habitats to suit the needs of agriculture and tourism, that the land, which was meant to be a biodiverse home for all sorts of creatures, is no longer as hospitable as it should be. Half a million natural ponds in the UK have been lost over the last 100 years, according to the Wildlife Trust. Half a million! My understanding of being a good host is that hospitality involves grace in making space for all sorts of vulnerable life, human, flora and fauna, to thrive. For me, the pond is a small symbol of trying to be a good, hospitable 'ruler' of all living things (Genesis

1:28), a ruler who tries to rule how God would rule. This means compensating for the damage my species has done to the homes of others by doing what I can to create a new safe space for them. It means being hospitable to the unwelcome guests to my pond as well as the dragonflies and damselflies. And one day, perhaps, a newt will appear and my joy will be complete. Messy Church has always had hospitality at its heart, as we make a safe space for all sorts of people to come together as the church family. Messy Church Goes Wild extends this hospitality in a new dimension and invites us to discover what it means to be good hosts to all life and good guests on a planet where God is the ultimate host.

Second, the walled garden. This is a centuries-old vicarage vegetable garden, bounded on three sides by a wall and fenced in along the lane edge, just opposite our house and the church. Fancifully, Charlotte Brontë probably ate potatoes grown in it when she visited her friend Ellen Nussey in the vicarage in 1845 and got the idea for *Jane Eyre* (though maybe not from the potatoes). Leaning on your fork, you get a delightful view down the valley towards Stanage Edge, about a mile away. A few decades back, the vicar invited various villagers to use it rather like an informal allotment and take over a patch to grow their own vegetables and fruit. Since then, gardeners have come and gone and herbs, rhubarb, beans, raspberries and onions flourish in the hands of retired people, young families and single people who have no garden of their own.

It's scruffy, as is the way with works in progress: there are sheets of old swimming-pool lining stopping the weeds and some rickety (but fiendishly effective) compost bins. My little patch has sprouted a crop of viper's bugloss, which was thick with bees all summer, and beans, a gift from one of the gardeners locally, as was a marrow plant. During lockdown, the 'tenants in the vineyard' came and worked their plots, escaping from their imprisonment at home, finding healing in their care for the land from the traumas they were going through and the side-by-side companionship every allotment gardener recognises.

However, the church feels the need for more space for parking, so there is talk of reappropriating the garden and putting down a meshed hard surface so that cars can be parked there. This raises the question of the responsibilities of ownership. Leaving aside the complexities of whether the land belongs to the diocese or the church (or indeed the vicar), the situation has to make us wonder about our responsibilities as 'owners' to 'to do good or to do evil, to save life or to kill', as Jesus asks in Mark 3:4 in the context of what the sabbath is all about *really*. In the case of the walled garden, the church effectively has the power over what happens to it. In the case of Messy Church, God has entrusted each Messy Church team with the power to shape what happens in that Messy Church: 'to do good or to do evil, to save life or to kill'. The opportunity and privilege is to keep on searching for how to make the absolute most of every opportunity, to take a space and create the most amazing, phenomenal, miraculous environment our imaginations are capable of. For the walled garden, this could be a car park. Or it could be a community orchard, an outdoor worship space, a spot for a firepit and community gatherings and open-air concerts. For a Messy Church, it could be about incorporating care for the planet into all we do, shaping the space into something even more beautiful. As Jesus' parables about tenants and rulers hint, with power over a household, vineyard or kingdom comes responsibility. And part of Messy Church's responsibility as the owner-tenants of a movement is to be responsible about the way we tread on the earth.

Lastly, a reflection on Easter morning 2021. Apart from the actual getting out of bed, I have always enjoyed dawn services on Easter mornings, but there was no tradition of this in the new church. So I set off on my own in the dark to walk up the valley and scramble up onto Stanage Edge to watch the sun rise. There were about ten people scattered around the boulders with a similar idea, all standing still and separate. We waited chillily as the light grew and grew, then exploded from the horizon in the east. It was glorious. It bellowed silently about a new day, a new life, new beginnings, darkness to light and transformative resurrection power. And I walked back home again.

My observation is hard to articulate because it's about mystery and by definition doesn't lend itself to a verbal explanation. It runs something like this: the world – the natural world – is shouting about God. In Messy Church we want to make opportunities where more people are able to hear these shouts and to respond in ways that draw them closer to Jesus. I would have loved to walk through the darkness alongside other Christians of all ages, just as the women went to Jesus' tomb in the early morning together – it would have been a shared experience rather than a solo one and would have been richer for it. But part of the joy lay in the fact that it was spontaneous and unstructured, rich in meaning and completely unpinned down by the normal scaffolding we build around communal worship experiences: instruments, liturgies, sung songs, spoken prayers, read-aloud scripture. As Messy Church goes wild, I want to find out more about what it means to worship the risen Jesus in and through the creativity of creation. This book is just the start.

In it, you'll find plenty of thought-provoking and informed passion to help us as individuals, as Messy Church communities and other intergenerational communities to understand more and take more action together to become more the people God calls us to be towards the planet.

In Part I we are challenged by seven experienced writers and practitioners to consider in depth what our response could be towards different aspects of the created world. George Lings muses on the concept of wildness in the very values of Messy Church. Dave Bookless leads us through an in-depth reflection on animals and birds in the Bible and beyond. Graham Hartland, one of the *Messy Church Does Science* authors, asks the apparently simple question, 'Why bother with plants?', and answers it with infectious enthusiasm and knowledge. This book's godmother, Jane Leadbetter, explores the oceans and seas and the problem of plastics that end up there, but offers achievable alternative actions and habits to cultivate in everyday life in response to the problem. Dave Gregory, a climatologist, helps us think through climate change and how we can behave differently to make a difference. From the USA, Crystal Goetz challenges us to love our neighbours – God's Messy people – in a rich variety of ways. Rachel Summers, from her rich experience of being outside with children and families, encourages us to slow down and notice more of the world around us and to follow the example of children in the way we relate to it.

In Part II, we enjoy stories from Messy Church leaders from different parts of the world as they reflect on their own Messy experience and story, some with case studies and some with the environmental considerations of a particular aspect of Messy Church or family life. These accounts are almost certain to spark off ideas for new approaches in your own context.

Finally, Martyn Payne and the Young Messy Leaders team offer two worked-out sessions for exploring wildness in your own Messy Church or other intergenerational setting. We are deeply grateful to all the contributors to this book for making it such a delightfully biodiverse set of writings!

PART I

MESSY ISSUES

1

Messy Church – wild at heart

George Lings

 After 22 years of parish ministry, George worked for Church Army from 1997 to 2017 directing its Research Unit, publishing stories and statistics of young churches. His long-time membership of the Northumbria Community fostered his BRF book *Seven Sacred Spaces*. He is married to Helen and they have five grandchildren. His hobbies include skiing, cycling and a model railway of a Derbyshire 1938 location.

What do you mean by 'wild'?

I wonder how you react when you read the word 'wild'? It's a word that can evoke very different feelings. It could be fear of things out of control and 'gone wild' – whether that is the untended garden rather inconveniently 'going back to nature' or, more worryingly, being with a person who is raging with anger or gone off on one, or even the unwelcome surprise that the pet dog has suddenly bitten you! Wild here is bad, to be resisted and brought back under control.

But the reaction to wildness could equally be awe at being in the splendid grandeur of a wild landscape that cuts us down to size, or a wildflower in bloom which protests to you that it really doesn't deserve to be called a weed. It could be delight during a David Attenborough programme watching the impressive life of a wild animal at home in its environment, being the glory it was always intended to be.

It could be more of an inner reaction – like a wild hope growing within you, as a passion for something you value looks like it might really happen. Wild here is good, to be honoured and its freedom respected. Sometimes it just isn't clear. Was the American 'Wild West' good or bad – or both mixed together?

Knowing that variety of meanings and reactions, this chapter argues that Messy Church Goes Wild should not be understood to mean that Messy Church used to be tame and safe, and has now got dangerous. Nor does it simply mean that Messy Church has joined the green movement and wants to care for the planet and all life on it. But as the title of this chapter, 'Wild at heart', implies, Messy Church has always had an element of wildness at its very core. That is when that word 'wild' is understood in the positive sense and when it rightly presents a wake-up call to other ways of being church that are so tame that, to mix a metaphor, they have gone stale. And 'tame' is another of those words whose meaning so depends on context; a tame dog can be such a delightful companion, whereas a tame husband is bound to be a disappointment!

Where am I coming from?

I write unashamedly as a Messy Church fan. I am convinced that it is both missionally effective and ecclesially creative. Equally important, it is no accident that those two factors are linked. Healthy wildness always reveals a balanced, interdependent relationship between a wild creature and its environment. So here, the creative values within a genuine Messy Church community connect with, and make sense to, those people it relates to in a mission context. For example, the quality of hospitality makes newcomers feel genuinely valued and treated well, or the creativity which is playfully welcomed unlocks that aspect of being made in the image of God that is in all of us.

I am also grateful to have been a small part in advocating that the best way to cooperate with the genius of Messy Church is to know and live out its values. Then we can be flexible, confident and even relaxed about how these values will work out in practice, knowing that different contexts will need different interpretations. It is similar in the evolution of species in the wild, as the swimming iguanas, or the diverse finches, on the set of islands of the Galapagos illustrate.

I also write as a companion of the Northumbria Community and monthly, while in prayer, I am met by the words of the poet Joel McKerrow:

> *As the tamed horse still hears the call of her wild brothers*
> *And as the farmed goose flaps hopeful wings as her sisters fly*
>   *overhead*
> *So too, perhaps, the wild ones amongst us*
> *are our only hope in calling us back to our true nature.*
> *Wild ones who have not been turned to stone*
> *by the far-reaching grasp of the empire*
> *and its programme of consumer sedation,*
> *the killing of imagination.*
> *Where, my friends, have the wild ones gone?*[1]

For years I have felt and mourned the captivity of the world, in which I too live, to the sovereignty of economics, lured by the evangelism of advertising that keeps our addictions refuelled and the delusion that 'the bottom line' is the most important thing. Equally I lament the disconnection of the church from society, the shame of our flawed history, our inward-facing preoccupations, our distaste for enthusiasm, earnestness and evangelism and our repeated insistence that what we face is not a major crisis. I am intrigued that the pandemic has challenged a view that the heart of being the church means a focus on being in a special building, on a Sunday, with people like us, to be spoon-fed with all we need from a person at the front. All this has been blown out of the water.

This machine has, for a time, ground to a halt, and I hope will be replaced by something more organic and less mechanistic, managed and centrally controlled. I hope for a kind of rewilding that puts Jesus – God's wild one – back in the driving seat. Reflecting on the rewilding metaphor, my friend Catherine Askew of the Northumbria Community paints a humorous and poignant parable of us and Jesus on a journey, in which we say that we so love him that we have put him in the favoured front passenger seat and tell him we look forward to his company as we drive along. However, he thanks us for our kindness, reminds us that it is his car, we are travelling his way and the passenger seat is reserved for us, and says, 'So take your hands off the steering wheel.' We are not to be in control. It happens that the pandemic has harshly reminded us of that.

Wildness and Messy Church values

I suggest that there is a healthy wildness at the heart of Messy Church, as defined by its values. In case any reader doesn't know them by heart, five values were publicly named over ten years ago. Being **Christ-centred** and **all age** were seen as the twin cores, expressed in three other values: **hospitality**, **creativity** and **celebration**.[2] I think we should connect them to another value which runs beneath and informs the delivery of the official five values. I mean the word **messy**. This is neither a licence for slipshod leadership, nor merely a comment on what happens when you mix children and creativity. This value calls for a humility which recognises that all our lives are messy. Therefore unconditional acceptance and a warm welcome to fellow flawed humans beckons, not the expected judgmental face of the church. Valuing mess gladly accepts that creativity will rightly overflow desires for mere tidiness. It will be relaxed when food or drink gets spilt during a meal because hospitality and humour are more important than a pristine tablecloth. It will be relaxed when a planned celebration isn't pitch-perfect, when a cue is missed and worship is genuine but flawed. In all those ways, it is so helpful and liberating to live well with messiness. I base this relaxed view on the spirit of 1 Corinthians 13 that even our best efforts are only good in part and that doing them out of love is a greater good.

In what ways do these values link to a healthy wildness? I start with **Christ-centred**. Back in 2004, Alison Morgan wrote a book called *The Wild Gospel*.[3] Its first three chapters explored the wildness of Jesus. He healed when he shouldn't, welcomed people others wouldn't, broke the rules of the day and insulted those guarding them. His wildness modelled a new style of leadership and even reshaped current views of God. It was a new way of seeing and a new standard of living – the sermon on the mount. He offered invitation into a new world, the kingdom of God. It was all very Galilean, known as a hotbed of revolutionaries. In the end it cost him his life. But then being raised from the dead is pretty wild too. That's Jesus the wild one. Seek being Christ-centred and these sorts of links with wildness beckon. Interestingly, recent research done by Church Army's Research Unit (CARU) underlines innovative and practical ways in which Messy Church leaders are following through this desire to be Christ-centred.[4]

I realise that, if challenged, nearly all churches would claim that value, and doubtless there are shining examples of it. However, there are too many church communities that are church-building centred, weighed down by the burden of finance to maintain their building and pay service-takers, and fixed on retaining historic styles of worship and church music. Here, wildness is miles away and even suspect.

Research data confirms Messy Church as living out the widely inclusive value of being **all age**. Both David Voas in *From Anecdote to Evidence* and Clare Dalpra and John Vivian in *Who's There?* showed that on average Messy Churches had three times as many under-16s as inherited churches.[5] Today there are many churches with few to no children.[6] That is not just bad news for the future of the church, but also a consequence of centuries of the separation out of children, sent out quickly to Sunday school or suppressed into 'being seen and not heard' in church. What a contrast to the view 'to be with children is to refresh your soul', or Jesus' teaching on having childlike attitudes (Matthew 18:3–4). Lucy Moore herself argues the case for, and handles the practicalities of, being all-age in her book on the topic.[7] How is this wild?

Could it be that children are themselves a keystone species for the church, bringing back factors that overpopulation by adults has excluded? I see here links to the quality of playfulness.[8] Children are at home in play and invoke the rediscovery of play in older people. I deeply enjoy being a grandparent to younger children and have had many happy hours absorbed with them in their games, freed from the cares of this world, entertained by the surprising connections they make and prizing the pearls they come out with. A bit of adult humility is in order here. As Antoine de Saint-Exupéry observes in his curious extended parable *The Little Prince*: 'Grown-ups never understand any-thing by themselves, and it is tiresome for children to be always and forever explaining things to them.'[9] The spontaneous nature of play also connects to the third value of creativity. Sadly, many churches struggle to be truly all age, let alone playful. Here is an aspect of wild-ness that can warm, not alarm. It is no accident that the 2019 research by Church Army Research Unit (CARU) into how Messy Churches are creating new spaces for faith was called *Playfully Serious*. They even pondered calling it *Seriously Playful*. I suspect that playfulness is another implicit value, like being messy. Both are like the wording that runs through a stick of seaside rock.

The value set on **creativity** permeates the entirety of a Messy Church gathering, not just the activity time. Creativity does occur in other churches, but seldom so widely across all attendees. The breadth of creativity in Messy Church stands in contrast to words too often linked to church services: boring and passive. Other criticisms of existing churches are of domination by both clergy and choirs. Related to this value of creativity is the notable liberating of many hitherto untrained lay leaders, especially women, through Messy Church, who come alive as their own creativity is unlocked. Both *Playfully Serious* and *The Day of Small Things* supply the data of this dynamic that should be char-acteristic of all people made in the image of a creator God.[10] The link to wildness is that in good rewilding diverse species are released, and better balance occurs across that diversity as each element plays its part – by being itself, and in that sense creative.

Messy Church **hospitality** begins with intentional welcome and runs all the way through to the dynamics of the meal. That Messy Church does hospitality better than many other churches is evidenced by the high proportion of non-churched people who come and then stay. On average 45% of their attenders have this background, much higher than in inherited church. Wise inherited churches have invested in welcome teams and meals at other times for newcomers, but stories still are told of poor welcome and the church being seen as an alien place. By making the shared meal normal, Messy Church has also revived the domestic angle of early Christian community. Following the legendary hospitality of the wild Jesus, true hospitality chooses to live with the unexpected, and even unwanted, guest. In the wild, surprise visitors to the watering hole are part of the delight.

Celebration is a much-used word for all sorts of services. Here Messy Church demonstrates wildness in that celebration genuinely occurs as the climax of the hospitality and the creative, and then flows into a meal which has its own sense of celebration. As such, this is more like a live show, whereas in inherited church the worship is usually the starting point, to which attenders come in cold. Moreover, church services are usually closely scripted and entirely pre-planned. The other contrast is after the dismissal, where in inherited church the refreshments are of variable quality and some brevity.

Behind all this there is another crucial element to healthy living with the wild. It is the issue of **control**. The rapid proliferation of Messy Churches was never tightly controlled by Lucy Moore, although BRF provides a steady stream of resources to aid them. The result is that there are both healthy and unhealthy Messy Churches; there are wilder and tamer ones. There are ones that exhibit the values and others that use the label but ignore the values. I immediately add that this mixed reality is true also of parish churches, as a number of parishioners and bishops know to their cost, despite books passionately arguing the virtues of the parish system. All expressions of church are easy to do badly and harder to do well.

My memory goes back to the 1950s, so I notice how society has become so risk averse. It is a temptation to think that we can and should control all outcomes. Back in 1993, John Cleese and Robin Skynner published *Life and How to Survive It*.[11] They argued that at the levels of family, organisations and society, an overemphasis on control denies people freedom to be creative, destroys trust and ends up being unhealthy for all. They don't use the word 'wildness', but they do rejoice in playfulness.

So how can taking risks be at the same time safe and wild? Lucy Moore has a delightful image. She commented to me that if you really know the steps in a barn dance or ceilidh, you don't become a dull, regimented automaton, you become freer, even a bit wilder – you begin to improvise within the framework. Something similar occurs in playing jazz. Structure is the friend and base for the spontaneous. If you live the values, you can relax and see what happens.

I've argued that Messy Church at heart has a degree of wildness. It doesn't *go* wild; it always has been. Some of the values are wild in themselves, for they prioritise following the wild Jesus; others deliberately take risks, as in creativity and hospitality. Then leaders live with having a trust in trust. They depend on God being God and knowing that true life comes from his intervention and creativity, not our machinations and industry. Not for nothing do they value the wind of the Spirit, that blows with a wildness in which we neither know where it comes from or where she may take us.

Why I care about the planet

I care about the planet because there is only one earth. All animals should have the right to live as long and as healthy as we can. Due to climate change Greenland is chipping away. We should love the world God made for us, gave to us, created for us.

Maisie, aged 9, Durham Diocese Youth Council

2

Caring for animals and birds

Dave Bookless

 Revd Dr Dave Bookless is director of theology for A Rocha International. A Rocha works in practical conservation across over 20 countries, and runs the EcoChurch programme (ecochurch. arocha.org.uk). Dave is also a part-time vicar, serves on various global committees, speaks and writes widely on creation care and loves spending time outdoors.

Caring for pets and wildlife comes naturally to many young children. Whether hamsters, rabbits or goldfish; cats, dogs or exotic pets; there's a deep delight in nurturing and being responsible for the well-being of another living creature. Many primary schools have incubators where eggs are hatched and chicks nurtured, as children learn about the wonders of life. And, of course, Noah's ark makes a fantastic children's Bible story, with animals, rainbows, mild threat and yet a happy ending.

Yet, the 'grown-up gospel' we teach in our churches and reveal in our mission priorities often says nothing at all about animals and birds. It's as if caring for our fellow creatures is a childish fad we're taught to grow out of. Therefore, it is important to understand how caring for animals and birds fits into the Bible's big story; how actually this is far closer to God's priorities than we often realise, and is an area where, to enter the kingdom of God, we need to become like and learn from children (Mark 10:14–16).

The Bible's big story (how we present the gospel) is often simplified to three main points:

- God made it all good.
- We've sinned and messed it up.
- Jesus offers us forgiveness and salvation.

In this framing of the story, 'creation', including animals and birds, appears at the beginning, but is left behind as the focus turns entirely to human sin and salvation. A much more biblical way of looking at the gospel, God's good news, is to present it not as a set of propositions, but rather as the big, true story that God invites us to be part of; a story that runs from creation to new creation. In this story, we humans are important but it's not just *our* story; it is God's story and includes plenty of other characters too, including animals and birds. They are part of God's plan and purpose from beginning to end, and the natural affinity to fellow creatures that many children have is not childish, but rather deeply connected to how God has hardwired us in a world of incredible variety and beauty.

Let's dip into God's big story to see what this means for how we treat our fellow creatures and how we can draw out these themes in Messy Church:

All very good: Right at the start we see God's delight in creativity, making a purposeful and ordered universe and filling it with an extraordinary diversity of creatures. At regular intervals, God stops to enjoy creation, declaring it 'good'. When complete, God looks at all that he's made and declares it all 'very good' (Genesis 1:31). This 'very good' includes humans but also includes all biodiversity – the variety of living things on earth. Interestingly, the Bible has no word for 'biodiversity' or even 'nature'. All of it, including both human and nonhuman creatures, is 'the work of God's hands'. Later in the Bible, Paul writes that 'since the creation of the world God's invisible qualities – his eternal power and divine nature – have been clearly seen, being understood from what has been made' (Romans 1:20).

Reflection and activity ideas

Where can we see God's power and nature in the work of God's hands? Encourage families to think about and draw or make collages of their favourite creatures (pets, wildlife, insects, even plants and trees) and to express what they learn about God's character from them. What does a dog teach about God? Let them enjoy the wordplay! Perhaps loyalty, love, joy – wagging tail; delight in physical exercise). How about cats? Maybe beauty, independence, playfulness. What about elephants, tigers, dolphins, hedgehogs, oak trees…? Another activity is to brainstorm ideas on what God is like (strong, loving, creative, relational) and then allow people to create their own imaginary animals that say something about God, using modelling clay, playdough or collage, or cut out pictures from magazines. Like Adam in Genesis 2, let them think of names for their animals.

The first commandment: Jesus said the greatest and first commandment is to love God with our whole selves, and the second is to love our neighbours as ourselves (Matthew 22:37–39). These may be first and second in importance, but God's first command in creation is all about how we treat our fellow creatures. In Genesis 1:28, God tells humankind to increase in number, subdue the earth and rule over the fish, birds and animals. This verse has often been misinterpreted to permit human domination and exploitation of nature. In fact, the text and context make it clear that humans are closely linked to other animals. God makes us on the same day (1:24–28) and like the animals we're made from the land (1:24, 2:7; the name 'Adam' derives from *adamah*, the Hebrew for earth or soil). Importantly the word for 'rule' or 'have dominion', *radah*, relates to the biblical idea of kingship, where rulers were to serve and protect their people. Jesus, as the 'servant king', is our model. We are to be guardians and encouragers of our fellow creatures, not 'lords and masters'. To bear the image of God (1:26–27) is to reflect the character of a God who creates in love and rejoices in creation's variety. This is spelled out in Genesis 2:15 where God sends Adam into the garden to tend and keep, or serve and preserve, the garden and its wildlife.

Reflection and activity ideas

How does loving God and neighbour relate to creation care? I've found that if you ask a group of children 'Who is my neighbour?' or 'Who should we care for?', animals come right after family in their answers. We did an activity craft project on this in our church and most responses were about saving whales and seabirds from plastic waste, picking up litter, planting to help pollinators or making bee and bug hotels (Air Bee & Bee!). All of these could be activities linked to what it means to *radah*, or care for, our fellow creatures. One important thing to emphasise is that we're animals too! Children have often picked up (from where?) the idea that humans are different from animals, but both biologically and biblically we are animals too – created on the same day from the land/earth. So, the leadership we show as those made in God's image is about leading from within, not from above.

All aboard the ark: Noah's ark is far more than a cute children's story. It talks about God's priorities in a time of ecological chaos, judgement and salvation and – guess what? God's not only interested in saving humans! Here is a message for our era of climate chaos and biodiversity loss. There were only four pairs of humans on the ark, yet seven pairs of most animals and birds, and even one pair of animals that were unclean, inedible or dangerous. God's reason for preserving wildlife was not for us to enjoy but simply 'to keep their various kinds alive throughout the earth' (Genesis 7:3). In other words, animals and birds matter because they are valuable to God, not because they matter to us. Moreover, when God makes a covenant through the rainbow, it includes not only people but 'every living creature' (9:8–17), a theme that the Hebrew text repeats seven times. Here we have a God who is passionate about biodiversity conservation and wants to prevent unnecessary extinction. Noah's ark and the subsequent covenant blow apart our narrow idea that salvation is only for humans, and challenge us to look urgently at what's happening to wildlife today. Since 1970, 70% of wildlife populations have disappeared globally,[12] and we are seeing the sixth global extinction event, this time not caused by ice ages, volcanoes or asteroids, but by us.

Reflection and activity ideas

See how much families already know about threats to wildlife (climate change, deforestation, overfishing, habitat loss and change, industrial farming, pollution including plastics and pesticides). See what they already know about species that are threatened both globally (polar bears, rhinos, pangolins – the most illegally-trafficked animal) and more locally (bees, skylarks, hedgehogs, stag beetles). Why not encourage a project, such as making posters or sending pictures and letters to politicians about threats to wildlife? Emphasise that these creatures matter to God. It's been said that every extinction erases a unique fingerprint of God. Why not write prayers of lament and sorrow at what we've done? Encourage action that is both global (e.g. supporting A Rocha's campaign to protect the Atewa forest in Ghana)[13] and local (creating 'Air Bee & Bee' bug hotels or bird boxes in a churchyard, or writing to your church/council about leaving unmown areas for wildlife).

God cares for the creatures. So should we! Genesis lays foundations, but the whole Bible shows God's care for animals and birds as well as people. In Psalm 145:9–10 we read, 'The Lord is good to all; he has compassion on all he has made. All your works praise you, Lord; your faithful people extol you.' Animals and birds praise God too, and God shows compassion – gentle, loving care – towards all creatures. So should we! God gives every creature the breath of life and provides food for them (Psalm 104:27–30), even in places where no humans live (Job 38:25–27). He knows and delights in all kinds of creatures (Psalm 50:9–11; Job 39:1–30). Sometimes animals and birds know God's ways better than us! In Numbers 22:21–35 God uses a donkey to speak to Balaam; in Jeremiah 8:7 migrating birds follow God more closely than people; in Job 12:7–10 we're invited to listen to birds, animals and fish to understand God's ways, and in Proverbs we're encouraged to learn from ants (6:6) and also rock badgers, locusts and lizards (30:24–28). No wonder Jesus urged us to look at the birds and the flowers to understand God better and not worry so much (Matthew 6:25–30).

Reflection and activity ideas

Animal cruelty is a sensitive but important subject to explore. People may not be aware of where their food comes from or how farmed animals are treated. It may not be appropriate to use shocking images of factory farming, but you could use Q&A and then a collage flow-diagram to explore what our favourite foods are and where they come from. When talking about meat, emphasise God's compassion and that God notices when a single sparrow falls (Matthew 10:29; a literal translation suggests God falls to the ground at the death of even the commonest creature). Why not have a veggie meal for Messy Church, or at least a veggie option?

Jesus and animals: During Jesus' 40 days in the wilderness we read, 'He was with the wild animals' (Mark 1:13). The wording suggests peaceful companionship rather than threat and builds on Old Testament ideas of wisdom and on prophecies that the coming Messiah would restore shalom, harmonious relationships, with God, people and wild creatures (Isaiah 11; 35; 40:3–5; Hosea 2:18). Whereas Adam and Eve's sin caused removal from the harmony of Eden, here the new Adam, Jesus, lives peacefully with wild creatures. In fact, throughout

Jesus' teaching and life, the gospels demonstrate his deep awareness of and closeness to nature, including animals and birds. God's kingdom (the New Testament's vision of shalom – restored relationships) includes learning from birds and flowers, foxes, fig trees, mustard seeds and the rhythms of planting and reaping. This isn't coincidence. The Bible is clear that Jesus himself is creator and sustainer of all life on earth (Colossians 1:15–17) and his death and resurrection restore all the relationships broken by sin. Jesus is not just our personal Saviour; he is Saviour of the world.

Reflection and activity ideas

There are some complex theological concepts here! One way to address that with children is with the simple question: 'How big is your Jesus?' Create a huge paper or card outline of Jesus (perhaps with his arms out, as in the Christ the Redeemer statue in Rio de Janeiro). Using magazine pictures, drawings, flowers, grass and anything else suitable, fill the outline of Jesus with animals, birds, mountains and rivers, not forgetting people and towns too. Use Colossians 1:15–20 as the heart of a time of worship to Jesus as Lord of all creation.

Animals and birds in the new creation: 'Will my puppy go to heaven?' is one of the hardest questions to answer. In truth, we don't know if every creature that's ever existed will be part of eternity, but we can be confident that animals and birds are definitely in God's new creation. Remember, when the Bible talks about 'new' creation or 'new' heavens and earth, it does not mean that God destroys this current creation but rather that creation will be radically refined, repaired, restored, renewed… even recycled (Acts 3:21; Romans 8:21; Revelation 21:5)! Both Old Testament visions (Isaiah 11:6–9; 65:25) and the book of Revelation (5:13) speak of animals and birds praising God eternally. Some think the four living creatures in Revelation 4 represent humans, domesticated animals, wild animals and birds, all worshipping Jesus.

Just as the Bible's big story began with God creating biodiversity and delighting in it, continues with God sustaining and caring for wild creatures and climaxes with Jesus dying to save 'all things in heaven and on earth' (Colossians 1:20), so eternity includes Father, Son and Holy Spirit worshipped by animals and birds as well as people.

Reflection and activity ideas

Think of all creation worshipping God, both now and eternally. How does a dog worship? Maybe tail wagging, barking or running across a field? How do trees worship? They 'clap their hands' (Isaiah 55:12), provide shelter, bear good fruit... What about birdsong? Be sure to include autumn and winter as well as spring and summer. How do decaying leaves worship God? By nurturing new life. This could lead to getting people to help write and illustrate a new version of the Benedicite,[14] an ancient hymn of all creation's worship (based largely on Daniel 3 and Psalm 148). The usual format is: 'Bless the Lord' and 'Sing his praise and exalt him forever!' There's a wonderful Tanzanian Benedicite in the 2019 Season of Creation pack.[15] Another activity could build on the idea that the new creation is a recycling of our current world: create a wonderful world, brimming with wildlife, rivers, forests and people, entirely out of recycled materials.

As we've seen, caring for animals and birds is right at the heart of the Bible's big story. Today we live in a nature-impoverished world, and it's getting worse fast. In *Last Child in the Woods*, Richard Louv argues many children today suffer from 'nature deficit disorder'.[16] Through Messy Church we can re-awaken the natural delight in creation that God has placed in our hearts. As we look at animals and birds, we discover a God who loves beauty, variety, interdependence and humour. We learn that we are one part of the great community of creation God has made, and that we have a special calling to be guardians and caretakers of our fellow creatures. Animals and birds teach us about trusting God, how to be wise, how to wonder, how to worship and how to work hard. We're invited to play our part in God's big story, knowing that one day Jesus will restore all things and that every creature in the sky, on land and under the soil will worship him too.

Why I care about the planet

I care about the planet as we need the earth for future generations such as our children and grandchildren. This is so important as we need somewhere that we know is safe and that we know is going to last for generations and generations. We also need to care about the planet for the species that live on it. Think... would you want you great grandchildren to have never seen an elephant or zebra? The amount of pollution in the air and in the sea is killing off animals on a daily basis. Humans being greedy and wanting more resources is leading to the cutting down of forests, which are vital to the survival of monkeys and gorillas. Over 20% of the Amazon rainforest has been cut down and a lot more is in danger as plans continue. The Amazon destruction has been held responsible for the extinction of 26 species of animals and plants. We need to save the planet, not just for us, but for our animals!

Evie, aged 14, Durham Diocese Youth Council

3

Caring for trees and plants

Graham Hartland

 Graham Hartland's passion for the natural world began inside Cornish rock pools and has flourished among the wild places of England, fuelling a shared ministry with his wife. In his spare time, he mixes storytelling and science as head of biology in a secondary school.

Plants are ubiquitous and often overlooked. Some of us may have good memories of gardening with grandparents, or of a window box of geraniums high up in a block of flats. Many of us would have encountered plants in school science lessons, with photosynthesis and osmosis taxing our teenage brains. In Messy Church, we may have been given a seed whose eventual growth was intended to illustrate some specific theological point. In this chapter, we'll look at a whole range of ways in which plants make our lives better and some of the creative ways in which humans have used plants. I'll also offer some suggestions for ways to give this whole area more thought in your church context.

So what is a plant? We know that plants are clearly not animals: they don't move or need distinct mealtimes, but beyond that many of us have little idea. We do know that plants need light and water – but not too much – and occasionally some fertiliser helps them to be greener and to flower and fruit better. Biologists will tell you that a plant has a cell wall made of cellulose and is green because of a pigment called chlorophyll. We will be familiar with these substances (whether we know it or not!) as cellulose is used to make Sellotape and chlorophyll is used to colour mint sauce. However, fungi (some of which we know as mushrooms) aren't plants, since they have no cellulose; nor are seaweeds (no complex cell types), sponges (an animal) or corals (again animals).

A tree is also difficult to define. While 'it gets wider each year and makes rings of wood' would be one definition, this excludes plants like bananas (classed as herbaceous as it has no wood), bamboo (a very big grass) and – somewhat ironically, having been made famous by the band U2 – the Joshua Tree (which is really a type of yucca, a succulent). It is safer, and more biologically accurate, to simply talk about 'plants' to save getting tangled up in confusing terminology. When God asked Adam to name creation in Genesis 2:19, you will notice that he only did it for the animals.

So why bother with plants? As a biology teacher in a secondary school, I am often faced with the long faces of students who find it difficult to relate to plants. Therefore we need to find things in common, just like in any relationship.

Food

Everything needs food, even plants. The difference is that plants make their own food, using carbon dioxide from the air, water from the soil and energy from sunlight. The scientists of ancient Greece considered these substances – air, water, soil/earth and energy/fire – to be the elemental bases of all life, and in a sense they are. Subsequent work has shown that these 'elements' are made of atoms of carbon, oxygen and hydrogen, and that energy isn't an element at all. Plants also need other substances – nitrogen, sulphur, iron, magnesium – to grow properly. These are combined with the carbon, oxygen and hydrogen to form their carbohydrates, proteins and fats – substances we understand as food. So as plants can feed themselves, they are the first organisms to colonise areas like bare rocks, beaches and cleared land. Other organisms, like animals, cannot make their own food from fresh air and water so gather what has been produced by plants for themselves. Herbivores like sheep and cows happily munch the leaves of fast-growing grass, and humans enjoy the lettuce and tomatoes in their BLT sandwich.

Sometimes plants work in cooperation with animals to their mutual benefit. Pollination, allowing the flowers of immobile plants to spread their genes more effectively, is achieved by paying the animal couriers with food. Plants pipe sugary juices to the flowers to form the nectar beloved of bees and butterflies, and indirectly to humans in the form of honey. The petals of magnolia trees are strong enough for the flowers to be pollinated by heavy beetles; mangoes, durians and agaves are robust enough for bats to pollinate them. Bizarrely, some plants like dodder have lost their ability to make their own food, so entangle and infect other plants like gorse and heather to steal theirs!

You might like to think about whether your faith community is one which has grown through positively interacting with the wider community it serves… or by feeding off other fellowships.

Humans, as animals, are able to eat a wide variety of plants. Our civilisations have grown around the cultivation of particular crops depending on location and climate. Arabia, Russia and Europe used wheat, oats and barley; India, southern Asia and China grew millet and rice; yam, cowpea and okra formed the basis for several African cultures; maize and beans were in Middle America, with addition of potatoes and quinoa in South America. Hunter-gatherer cultures will have a wider diet according to where they are and what is naturally in season. What we drink is made from or flavoured by plants like oranges, apples, tomatoes, mangoes, elderflowers, lemons, cacao, tea, coffee and sugarcane. Our social life might include drinks created by fermenting grapes, wheat, rice, barley or potatoes. Even to make a simple curry requires a blend of up to 14 different species of plants including cumin, coriander seeds and leaves, garlic, ginger, cinnamon, black as well as green cardamom pods and fenugreek. When I ask students about their own diets, we regularly find that over a week we consume products of dozens of different plant species. Without plants, there would literally and obviously be no food, and drinking plain water might be somewhat bland.

> You might consider whether you are giving your congregation a good diet of activities or whether it is the same old same old. 'People do not live on bread alone' has a multiplicity of interpretations.

Fuel

Plants burn well. Wood is used as a fuel for cooking as well as heating in many parts of the world. I'm writing this in April 2021, and the fragrant smokes of barbecues are filling the air as people's homes start opening up after the Covid-19 lockdown. The fuel for these is usually charcoal formed from the wood from coppicing – sustainable forestry – in Britain. Fire is also used for the farming technique of slash and burn, which is rightly pilloried for its indiscriminate and permanent destruction of forests for pastures and plantations. But 'shifting cultivation', which clears areas by rotation for farming within a forest much like coppicing, has been shown to work well in places like northern Thailand.

Waste crops can be turned into methane gas inside modern bioreactors. This echoes the situation millions of years ago when forests close to shores were overwhelmed by ocean waves and buried in sand. Overtime, they underwent a series of chemical changes and – depending on conditions – turned into rock or coal. If the former, then, as at Ynyslas Beach in Wales, the petrified forests can resurface; if the latter, the black lumps can sometimes retain the ghostly imprints of ancient tree ferns and giant dragonflies.

You might like to consider whether your faith community's use of plants and the energy derived from them is sustainable or whether you need to change what you do to reduce your carbon footprint.

Shelter

Perennial plants, those which live for longer than a year, provide shelter for other organisms. We may have come across moss growing in the moist cracks of trees; bromeliads and some orchids also adopt this strategy of using the high branches of plants as a location to grow. Animals also use plants as a place to live and shelter: hazel and holly clumps are good for ponies and cows to hide from Exmoor rains; gorse and heather make good nest sites for birds like Dartford warblers and stonechats; pine branches make anchor points for the webs of spiders; foxes excavate the sandy soil between the roots of beech trees; squirrels make their drays in tall oaks. Beavers create arrays of dams from willow or cottonwood trees and form both homes and food stores: the flood control offered by these structures has inspired humans to create artificial water management features, slowing the flow of water from heavier rains caused by climate change.

In 2011, a 77,000-year-old bed made by ancient humans was discovered in Sibudu, South Africa. Made of layers of grasses and sedges, it included aromatic laurel leaves which contained natural insecticides to ward off mosquitoes. Many plants have such chemicals for protection, and humans have used many of these as medicines. Foxgloves yielded digoxin, a variant on digitalis, for treating some heart conditions; the cancer-fighting medicines vincristine and vinblastine come from the Madagascan rosy periwinkle; willow bark has given us aspirin, once a routine painkiller and now used in select circumstances to reduce risk of heart attacks.

You might consider how you use the space around your faith community: are there enough living spaces to increase species numbers? What can you do to make the area more healthy?

Craft and building

Humans have learned how to shape the bodies of plants themselves: spruce trees form the trusses that hold up the roofs of homes in Europe and North America; teak builds homes in Thailand, while bamboo does a similar function in Bali; people in British Columbia build with lodgepole pines; walnut can be skinned to veneer furniture and used whole for firearms. Beech trees can be sliced to make floor planks and willow can be woven to make baskets and coffins. Tool handles are made from the springy woods of acacia, ash and hickory, allowing the dissipation of the striking force to reduce wear and tear on our bones. Some woods can be carved: visitors to old English mansions will marvel at the oak panels, and the gold standard carving of Grinling Gibbons adorns high statues in places like Windsor Castle and Hampton Court. Watching television programmes by Ray Mears inspired my son to take up spoon carving. In Wales, the lovespoon is a delightful way to celebrate the skills of a young man as well as his affection for his beloved.

The first boats were dug out from logs. Further additions like sails allowed the Tepukei vessels of the Santa Cruz islands to navigate across hundreds of miles of open sea to the Solomon Islands. Pulling these heavy craft up a beach after a trip required the coordinated work of lots of people; songs were used to keep everyone motivated and organised. Sea shanties, so beloved by many in the UK, were used to do the same thing. After the UK Covid-19 lockdown was lifted during spring 2021, one thing churchgoers commented on was the relief of being able once more to sing together during services.

You might consider whether you are creating opportunities for people to express their craft skills in your faith community.

Music

On the note of music, blowing across and through handheld grass stalks have been used for centuries as signs and signals. Ts'ai Yen's '18 verses sung to a Tatar Reed whistle' dates from around AD200, while modern children might use such to create squeals and screams during playtime. Twisting plant fibres can make strings, but these are easily broken, which is why we usually only see plants being used as the bodies of wind and percussion instruments. Gourds, related to pumpkins and squash, come in a variety of forms. As such, they are used as resonators in stringed instruments like the kora of Gambia and Senegal or the sitar of India. In Hawaii, the ipu hokiokio and the 'ohe hano ihu are nose-played whistles and flutes, while the ukeke, a musical bow, uses the mouth as a resonator. All three were used for entertainment, especially in courtship. Flutes and recorders are easily made by drilling holes in stems; shawms use the flexible properties of reeds to add a more nasal sound to a flute, and this led to the development of oboes and clarinets. Saxophones result from Adolphe Sax's work: he wanted an instrument which combined the flexibility of the bass clarinet with the punch of brass instruments like trumpets.

Drums have developed over millennia from their origins in banging hollow logs. In South Africa, Venda drums are made by using fire and axe to hollow out a tree before covering it with a whole cow hide. One was played by Nelson Mandela at the opening of the World Summit on Sustainable Development in Johannesburg in 2002. Trees outside the tropics show obvious growth rings. Warmth and abundant light give rise to speedy growth and thus wide rings; colder and drier weather slows the growth, and thus the rings narrow. The resultant pattern of rings of different widths can be read like a bar code. Reading and interpreting these bar codes is called dendrochronology and allows us to date timbers as well as giving a history of the climate around a tree over hundreds of years. Research published in 2013 uses the oak and pine trees from central Europe to produce an accurate chronology going back to 10500BC. This allows us to date archaeological artefacts as well as note the effects of climate change. For example, large volcanic eruptions slow tree growth in the summer and 2018 research in the Qinghai-Tibetan plateau showed the effect of these over 400 years.

> You might consider the effects of your faith community on the lives of the wider community. What signs of impact are there on yourselves as well as by yourselves?

Writing and painting

Music can often be accompanied by words. In early times, these scripts would simply have been memorised. Later on, writing was used: financial records and market trading making their first impressions in clay with stories like Gilgamesh following on. Ancient Egyptians then sliced papyrus into sheets which were bound to make scrolls, while in China a similar thing happened to bamboo. This was later replaced by paper: mulberry tree bark was pounded and formed into a sheet, with hemp rags and old fish nets being added to create a higher-quality product. The earliest records date this to AD105. Writing and painting was added using inks and paints. Paints can be made from crushed stones, but many of our natural colours originate from strongly coloured plants like beetroot, carrot, yarrow, walnut husks, lavender, blueberries, spinach and blackcurrants. The range of colours and inks obtained allows us to communicate in a variety of ways: short, scribbled notes and graffiti, the indigo tie and dye fabrics of West Africa, Chinese landscape paintings, Arabic calligraphy, Shakespearean sonnets: a long way from the 45,500-year-old painting of Sulawesi warty pigs found in Leang Tedongnge cave, whose discovery was announced in January 2021.

You might consider how you communicate within your faith community. Are the words and graphics accessible to all? As an example, a 20-year-old graphical art student in one of our congregations rebranded the church's advertising material using vibrantly coloured and gender- and age-neutral cartoon characters.

Clothing

Decorating ourselves with our clothes is also a use for plants. In Genesis 3:7 we are told that Adam and Eve, on becoming shamefully aware of their nakedness, sewed the relatively large leaves of the fig tree to form a scratchy and skimpy loincloth or apron. These thermally useless garments were replaced in Genesis 3:21 by the animal skins given by God, which are more hard-wearing as well as being substantially warmer.

Clothes production has come some way since then. While animal products like wool and silk are common, plant materials like cotton, hemp, bamboo and even nettles – the fibres, anyway! – can be used. Bark cloth can be made from the bark of mulberry and breadfruit trees; in a nice twist on the Genesis story, it can also be made from the bark of the Natal fig tree. This cloth is made by beating the inner bark to sheets and forms the traditional clothes of the Bugandan people of Uganda. Plant fibres can be mixed with those of various plastics like polyester to make them more hard-wearing. White clothes can be made more interesting by adding dyes: adding a mordant, like salt, fixes the dye to the fibres more firmly so it doesn't wash out.

Colour and scent

Colour is important when choosing flowers for decoration. Visitors to Hawai'i might receive a lei, a wreath of flowers. Proverbs 4:5–9 talks of loving Wisdom so that 'she will give you a garland to grace your head and present you with a glorious crown'. Such garlands made of colourful and fragrant flowers like jasmine and hibiscus adorn statues of Hindu deities; women wear a gajra – a garland – which includes scented flowers during festivals. The Kortha maalai, garlands intricately made using needles and thread and including jasmine, mullai and lotus, are a feature of south-Indian ceremonies. Children in England have long delighted in creating daisy chains. Wreaths at funerals and Christmas are common. In 2021 I saw my first Easter wreath, the daffodils being augmented by chocolate eggs, chicks and fluffy bunnies as other flowers were in short supply. Greater works of art are found in arrangements by a church's team or by professionals. Occasionally a flower festival is organised, where the colours, structures and smells of plants are combined to tell a story or develop a theme.

Our own smells can be augmented (or disguised) by perfumes, bought with considerable thought and more money. These are created by highly trained perfumiers from libraries of hundreds of scents, many of which come from plants. Likewise, the atmosphere of our buildings can be improved by air fresheners or scented candles. Sometimes incense can be burned. This is created from the bark or resin of various plants: ceder and boswellia being two used. Some churches, in common with other faith communities use it within worship: as Psalm 141:2 says it, 'May my prayer be set before you like incense; may the lifting up of my hands be like the evening sacrifice.' Carefulness with asthmatics might limit its use, as it can trigger an attack; that said, it is such a distinct scent that for some it conjures an atmosphere of peace and contemplation.

> **What is the scent created by your faith community? How does the fragrance of Jesus fill not just your space but the area around it?**

Health has three dimensions: social, physical and mental. Plants aid us in all three: socially, they cause people to come together to grow crops and celebrate festivals; physically, they feed us, make us better through medicines and keep us protected through clothes and buildings; and mentally, they enliven our creativity through carving, music, art, writing, colour and scent.

Action points

How many plants can you identify? We respect that which we know about and understand. As Christians, do we respect God's creation sufficiently to name its constituent parts and care for them? After all, in Genesis 2:15, the God-given first task of human beings was to work in the garden, and that was before the fall happened.

Clean the environment. Since bright light and unpolluted soil are necessary for plant growth, how clean is the area around you? How could you make it cleaner?

Plant crops and flowers and share the excess. Planting seeds always results in having too many, just like in the wild. Some places have garden clubs in which members swap, sell or donate their excess plants. Is there one in your area? Starting a garden might begin with donated seedlings.

Shop responsibly. Do you know where your food comes from? Is it a major source of water poverty in its area, like some cut flowers are in Uganda? Should you ask your local shops to buy locally? Is there a way of ethically sourcing food? Companies like Oddbox sell vegetables which are too big, wrongly shaped, superficially damaged or in excess and would otherwise go to waste and landfill.

Compost. While this can be difficult if space is at a premium, many areas have places where vegetable waste can be composted rather than left to decompose in landfill. Compost can be spread on soil, allowing nutrients locked up in dead plants to be transferred back to the earth and increasing its fertility.

4

Caring about plastics

Jane Leadbetter

 Jane Leadbetter was part of the BRF Messy Church team until December 2020. She has worked as a primary school teacher and was children's work adviser in the Diocese of Liverpool for twelve years. She runs L19: Messy Church once a month.

God works in mysterious ways. On my way home from a meeting, feeling angry after witnessing the plastic litter left behind, the amount of single-use plastic that had been purchased and the realisation that everyone in the room was thinking, 'Someone else will sort this problem, not me!', I spied a notice board advertising 'Liverpool's First Zero Waste Convention'. It was its final day, hours even, and I found myself parking up by Liverpool docks, shocked at my sudden decision to enter a new world of inspiration. The first person I encountered was Lucie, in the Ecobrick Zone. She listened to my anger and encouraged me to channel it into something positive. From that day I changed my language, my emotions, my challenges and expectations. Driving home after this zero-waste event, I felt a calling to help to save our planet. It wasn't to be done with anger and loud exclamations, though. It was to be a quiet and subtle mission, taking small steps at a time.

I am acutely aware, as I type this, that I am using a laptop, keyboard and mouse, which are all made out of plastic. I look beyond my laptop and see plastic stationery held neatly in a plastic box; plastic picture frames surrounding plasticised photographs; a plastic table mat to protect the table; and plastic pins holding important or dearly loved items to my notice board. I hold up my hands to declare that I am not plastic free! I am unlikely to ever be! But I hope that helping others to be more aware of alternatives, a change in lifestyle and having a strong voice can make a difference to society, our environment and the future of this planet.

'Plastic' is a word that originally meant 'pliable and easily shaped'. It is durable, hard-wearing, strong, lightweight, convenient and economical. Made from petrochemicals, the first man-made plastic made its first appearance in 1862 at the Great International Exhibition in London. It is only quite recently that plastic has become a name for a category of materials called polymers. Polymer means 'of many parts' and cellulose is a common polymer. The development of new plastics has provided endless possibilities. During World War II there was an expansion of the plastics industry in the United States, and with the need to preserve natural resources, producing synthetic alternatives became a priority. Nylon, invented in 1935, was used for parachutes and ropes. Plexiglas became an alternative to glass in aircraft windows. After World War II a surge in plastic production saw plastic taking the place of steel in cars, and paper and glass in packaging. Today there are thousands of plastic products. Hidden plastic can be found in tea bags, chewing gum, clothing, coffee cups, cigarette butts, disposable wipes, glitter, drinks cans, toothpaste, paint, on receipts, sewing thread, cardboard takeaway food containers, metal bottle caps, tampons and sanitary towels.

The plastic problem

We are causing plastic pollution. Yes – you and me, your family and friends, neighbours, school friends, work colleagues, in every country and continent! Not only is it ugly to look at, but it is harming animals and wildlife, damaging ourselves and making the climate worse. By 2050 there will be more plastic than fish in the sea. A full 100% of baby sea turtles have plastic in their stomachs and between 8 to 14 million tonnes of plastic waste enters our oceans every year. If you are reading this sitting on a beach in the UK, there are 5,000 pieces of plastic and 150 plastic bottles for each mile of beach. Off to purchase some fish and chips for a meal? One in three fish caught for human consumption contains plastic. You won't be able to see it without a strong microscope, but there are now 5.25 trillion macro and micro pieces of plastic in our oceans and 46,000 pieces in every square mile of ocean, weighing up to 269,000 tonnes.

Plastic breaks down, but it doesn't disappear. It gets smaller and smaller until it turns into tiny pieces, which end up in everything – the food we eat and the air we breathe. Our littering habits mean we clog up rivers and litter the deepest parts of our oceans, allowing it to get stuck in the stomachs of animals who mistake it for food. Micro-plastics contain harmful chemicals which are poisonous to wildlife and to us. My reusable water bottle is made out of plastic. I plan to use it for a very long time. But I need to remember to change the water inside regularly, as sunlight shining through the plastic bottle could make toxins in the plastic leach into the water. Clothes made from artificial materials shed microplastic fibres when washed. Microbeads, another type of microplastic, are sometimes added to products such as cosmetics, toothpaste and scrubs. Impossible to filter from waste water, they end up in our oceans. Plastic pollution has been found in Antarctica. Turtles, dolphins and seabirds can become entangled by plastic and injured or drowned. More than one million seabirds and 100,000 marine animals die from plastic pollution each year. The statistics are shocking.

So, now we know that plastic adversely affects not just the earth, but our own health too. Around 50% of plastic used is only used once. The amount of plastic waste in one year could circle the world four times. Plastic has been a protector during the Covid-19 pandemic, but it has also meant an increase in plastic medical waste, which will have long-term impacts on the environment. While Covid-19 will hopefully eventually go away, plastic waste will not. It is here forever. Has the pandemic plastic problem set us back even further?

What could we do?

We have all contributed to this plastic problem, mostly unknowingly, and it is our responsibility to take action to save the planet. God charged us with caring for the world: 'The Lord God took the man and put him in the Garden of Eden to work it and take care of it' (Genesis 2:15). As gardeners and caretakers, we have lost our role descriptions, enjoying the short-term ease of daily life by purchasing conveniently wrapped food and drink. But if we each used less plastic and found alternative ways to live our lives; if we each made different choices in the shops and stores so that manufacturers did not need to produce as much plastic; if we each used our voices to inform supermarkets and companies that we are unhappy with their plastic products, we could start to make a difference.

Recycling is worth it. Bottle-shaped plastics can be recycled: drinks bottles, detergent and shampoo bottles, milk cartons and home cleaning bottles. A plastic milk carton can be recycled into more milk cartons up to ten times. But each time, more polymers will be added to strengthen the plastic. It is a myth to think recycling is the solution to the plastic problem. Globally, only 9% of all plastic is recycled. The rest is burned in incinerators, goes into massive dumping sites or clogs up our streams, rivers and oceans. We still have far too much unrecyclable plastic produced. Lots of plastic packaging waste goes abroad, the equivalent of three Olympic-sized swimming pools every day.

We could just **stop using plastic bags**! A plastic bag is used for an average time of twelve minutes. More than 1 million plastic bags end up as waste every minute. The world uses over 500 billion plastic bags a year – that's 150 for each person on earth. Instead, use reusable shopping bags. The demand for plastic supermarket bags has been greatly reduced since the 5p charge was introduced in 2015, but the Bags For Life have become Bags For A Week! We have just shifted the problem.

Carry a reusable drink bottle. Plastic bottles make up a large part of plastic waste. 17 million barrels of oil are used to create 50 billion disposable water bottles in the United States alone. By using a reusable drink bottle, you could be saving your own money as well as helping the environment. Invite Messy Church families to bring named reusable bottles along to sessions. There are apps to show you where you can refill reusable bottles.

Avoid plastic packaging. This is hard to do in supermarkets, although some are offering loose wonky vegetables. A quarter of all domestic waste is food packaging. Try and find local shops for Messy Churches to adopt. Find a greengrocer and buy what you need loose rather than overbuy. Share this with other Messy Churches. Promote your local butcher, baker or greengrocer on your social media and increase their footfall. Create Messy Church certificates of endorsement for them. Invite different families to sponsor your Messy Church fruit bowl or breadbasket each month and share which shop you used with all the families. As more refill shops or zero-waste shops are opening, adopt them in your Messy Church life. Chat with local allotment holders. Find local farmers' markets.

Ditch plastic cutlery and straws. Invest in sporks and paper straws if straws are absolutely necessary. Invest in Messy Church washing-up teams. Value them by choosing an eco-friendly team name like Planet Pot Washers or Eco Warrior Washers. Use reusable dishes and celebrate how little is wasted. Join a Community Compost.

Avoid using cling film. It cannot be recycled and if heated may release chemicals. Use alternatives such as tin/aluminium foil, which can be recycled if clean. Crumple it into golf ball-sized balls. Plastic storage boxes and glass jars can be washed and reused. Beeswax wraps are great for wrapping sandwiches or paper sandwich bags. Reuse biscuit tins for keeping cakes fresh. Silicone food covers are great for keeping leftovers in Messy Church fridges. A plate is even better!

Find alternatives to plastic bottle toiletries, body products and household cleaning products. There are lots of plastic-free alternatives such as shampoo bars and eco-deodorant and -dental floss. Refill stores have shower and shampoo options too. Natural toothpaste and sun cream are now in abundance, and bamboo and wooden toothbrushes have long been available.

Recycle better. The recycling of plastics is so confusing. Different counties and authorities differ in their recycling information. For example, some councils will allow plastic yoghurt pots to be recycled. Others say no. Different authorities have different-coloured household recycling bins or boxes to others. Many recycling centres have to deal with waste that was put into recycling bins by mistake but will end up in the incinerator.

We could ask for **deposit return schemes**. Pay a little extra when we purchase a drink in a plastic bottle but then return the empty bottle to the shop to get your money back.

We could use our voices to **campaign for big companies to do more** to protect our environment. Recent child campaigners have successfully stopped some fast-food companies from producing plastic toys for children.

Reuse our plastic. Be creative and recycle plastic items into something useful or artistic. Plastic milk cartons make great bird feeders or watering cans. A plastic bottle can become a bee or bug hotel. We have lots of ideas on the Messy Church Pinterest boards.

Make ecobricks. One way to use plastic that cannot be recycled is to cut it into very small pieces and fill clean, dry plastic bottles. When these bottles are full and a desirable weight, they can be logged on GoBrik.com, where they receive a registration number. Lots of projects around the world are looking for really good, solid ecobricks to build with. By joining ecobricks together with silicone to create modules, tables and stools can be built, performance stages, benches and so on. Some countries are covering these kinds of constructions with cob and building playground equipment, shelters, churches and schools. Lots of schools hold ecobrick clubs. After asking pupils to collect household unrecyclable plastics for one week and, listening to how the process has impacted on the whole family, use it to create school stools, sheds and garden or vegetable planters. There are lots of ideas shared at ecobricks.org.

Choose clothing and other personal items which are made from earth-friendly materials instead of microfibres or synthetic fibres which pollute our water.

Pick up plastic litter when out walking or exercising. Always pack gloves and watch out for sharp objects.

Make green goody bags. Instead of making party bags with plastic yo-yos and toys plus plastic balloons, use home-made treats like fudge, eco-friendly note pads and packets of seeds.

Become a plogger! Plogging is a combination of jogging and picking up plastic litter. The craze began in Sweden in 2016 and now the United States has lots of plogger groups.

What WILL you do?

All of the above are important, but it can feel a bit overwhelming. You may feel that you can't even try to begin on your own. It is too big a mountain to climb. Is it important enough to get going on a plastics project? Who could you work with to make a difference? Well, pray about what lies heaviest on your heart about the plastics problem. Bring it to God and share your thoughts with him. Who knows how he may respond?

Some suggested action points:

- Talk with your Messy Church team about ways to reduce plastic in your sessions.
- Invite someone to talk at your celebration time about God's purpose for each one of us in caring about how we use plastics.
- Encourage church prayer groups to pray about plastic pollution in the environment.
- Include recycling plastic activities for all ages in your Messy Church sessions.
- Create and value a washing-up team.

At a recent ecobrick workshop in a primary school, I was challenged by a seven-year-old boy to stop poisoning his world. As adults, we have the bad habits, but it is not too late to try and change them and be better role models for the young. Remember the role descriptions given by God: gardeners and caretakers. Don't let plastic beat us.

Why I care about the planet

I think we need to stop using plastic because it is bad for all of the environment and it makes animals die. It is also making animals disappear and I wonder if we will see them ever again.

Farah, aged 7, Durham Diocese Youth Council

5

Caring about climate and weather

Dave Gregory

 Dave Gregory is a former research meteorologist and climate scientist. He now divides his time between being a minister at Croxley Green Baptist Church and exploring science, the environment and faith with churches, schools and community groups. A former Baptist Union president, he leads the Baptist Union Environment Network (BUEN) and is chair of The John Ray Initiative (JRI). As Dr Dave, he leads Messy Church Does Science and is working with the Messy Church team to take science outdoors in Messy Church Goes Wild Adventures.

Talking about the weather

Most people care about the weather – especially when it's so variable in the place you live that's it hard to know what it's doing from one day to the next. If you live in the United Kingdom, you will know talking about the weather is something we do all the time. It is often the next topic of small talk after greeting someone; 'Hello! How are you? Lovely/Terrible [*delete as appropriate*] weather we've been having.'

But even in the Bible, long, long ago, people were talking about the weather.

> [God] draws up the drops of water, which distil as rain to the streams; the clouds pour down their moisture and abundant showers fall on [humankind]. Who can understand how he spreads out the clouds, how he thunders from his pavilion?
> JOB 36:27–29

Elihu, who speaks these words, is a friend of a very troubled man, Job. Job has much in life to complain about, including the weather, for storms and strong winds played a part in his misfortune (Job 1:19). Elihu is incredibly good at observing the weather. He knows that water evaporates from the ground and forms clouds, which then produce rain that falls upon the earth. This is what scientists today would call the weather water cycle.[17] Still, Elihu realises there is much more to know: 'Who can understand how [God] spreads out the clouds?'

When I read these words, as a former meteorologist, I do so with a slight smile on my face. We might say in response to Elihu, 'Yes, we do understand the clouds.' Through God's wonderful gift of science, we can understand a lot about how weather works. We can write complicated computer programmes – so called 'computer models' – of how the atmosphere and ocean work. Using powerful supercomputers – like tens of thousands of laptops linked together – we can predict the weather several days and sometimes up to a week ahead.[18]

Given how complicated the weather is, our ability to predict it is astounding. But just as in Elihu's day, we must admit that we don't know everything. Our weather forecasts do go wrong, and I am sure that you have cause to complain when your outdoor Messy Church Goes Wild activity has been rained on again!

This reminds me of another conversation from the New Testament, between Jesus and Nicodemus, who, like Job, was struggling to understand how God participates in our lives and the world. In response, Jesus says, 'The wind blows wherever it pleases. You hear its sound, but you cannot tell where it comes from or where it is going' (John 3:8). Perhaps God too has a little smile on his face, for even with our scientific knowledge we need to remind ourselves that there is still a lot that we do not comprehend about the wonder of God's creation.

Talking about the climate

While we struggle to predict the weather beyond a week ahead, we can predict how the Earth's climate may change over the next 100 years. But wait, I might hear you say. How come we can predict the climate so far ahead and not the weather? Weather is what happens in the here and now, in one place or another. It changes day after day between sunny and cloudy skies, dry and wet days, heat waves and cold snaps. Climate is the average of the weather over time. So, while in the summer we cannot predict exactly what the weather will be on any day in the coming winter, we know that winter will be colder than summer. It is easier to predict this average temperature, because the Earth's climate is controlled by the balance of energy the Earth receives from the Sun and that which it loses to space, than the weather at any one time and place.

Climate does not just change through the seasons of the year. It also changes over the decades and centuries too. In the 21st century, climate is changing faster than at any time over the past 20,000 years. The past ten years have been the hottest the Earth has been since we began to take global temperature measurements 150 years ago.[19] And using tree rings to estimate temperate, we can say that it is hotter than the past 1,000 years.

Goldilocks and the greenhouse – a climate that is just right

It is often said that the Earth is just right for life because of the Goldilocks effect. It is at just the right distance from the Sun so that is it not too hot, nor too cold, but just right for liquid water to exist. But this is only part of the story – the atmosphere must be just right too.

When we stand outside and look up, the atmosphere above our heads seems huge. But the truth is that it is only a very thin layer of gas wrapped around our planet. If you want to get an idea of how thin it is, take an apple in your hand and take a bite from it. Look at how thin the skin is. If the Earth were the size of an apple, then the atmosphere would be about as thick as the apple's skin. But don't let that fool you. That thin layer of gas is responsible for warming the planet by 30 degrees centigrade. Without it, the Earth as seen from space would not be a planet of verdant, green-covered lands, sparling blue oceans and gleaming white clouds but a frozen white snowball spinning in space. The warming of the Earth by the atmosphere is called the greenhouse effect. Along with the Goldilocks effect, it is one of the wonders of creation that we should give thanks to God for. Without it, our lives, and the life of all living creatures on the Earth, would be very difficult if not impossible!

The atmosphere is a mixture of many different gases. Just under four-fifths (78%) is a gas called nitrogen, which is needed by plants to grow healthy and strong. Just over a further fifth (21%) is oxygen, the gas that we and animals need to produce energy from the food that we eat. About five parts in every 100 parts of the atmosphere (0.5%) is water vapour, while an even smaller amount – 400 parts in every 1,000,000 parts (0.04%) – is made up of a gas called carbon dioxide.

You might think that the gases that make up most of the atmosphere were the cause of the massive 30-degree centigrade warming that makes life possible on the Earth. But no. The way the atmosphere works is like the story Jesus told about planting a mustard seed: 'It is the smallest of all seeds, yet when it grows, it is the largest of garden plants and becomes a tree, so that the birds come and perch in its branches' (Matthew 13:32). Only an exceedingly small part of the atmosphere (water vapour, carbon dioxide and some other gases) causes the Earth to warm. We call these greenhouse gases.

So how does this work? Oxygen and nitrogen, along with the greenhouse gases, allow visible light – that which you can see with your eyes – from the Sun to pass through the atmosphere and warm the surface of the Earth, just like sunlight passes through the windows of your house. The warm ground and oceans also emit light – infrared light. Our eyes cannot see infrared light without using a special camera, although you can feel it with your hand if you place it next to the ground on a hot day. Oxygen and nitrogen let this 'heat' light travel through the atmosphere back into space. But the greenhouses gases trap some of this infrared light, causing the Earth to warm and be comfortable for life to flourish.

This is called the greenhouse effect because it's like the way a greenhouse lets light in but traps warm air inside, allowing plants like tomatoes, cucumbers and peppers to grow when they might struggle outside. Yet, I think it might be better to call it the duvet effect. Many people have thin summer duvets and then switch to a thicker one in winter to keep warmer. The atmosphere acts like a duvet covering the Earth. And because we have not been careful in the way we treat the atmospheric duvet, it is getting 'thicker' and the Earth warmer.

Hotter planet and wilder weather

For the past 200 years, we have been using fossil fuels – coal, oil and gas – to provide us with energy to run our cars and planes, to heat and light our homes, and power our TVs, computers and phones. Fossil fuels are the remains of plants and animals that lived millions of years ago. They have been buried under the ground, squeezed and heated to make the different types of fossil fuel that we rely on. They are made up of a lot of carbon, and when we burn them to make energy this combines with oxygen in the atmosphere to make carbon dioxide, one of the most powerful greenhouse gases. We have also been cutting down a lot of forests, which also releases more carbon dioxide into the air.

About half of the carbon dioxide that humans produce gets absorbed by plants, the soil and the oceans. The other half stays in the atmosphere and slowly builds up. Two hundred years ago, there were 280 parts of carbon dioxide in every 1,000,000 parts of the atmosphere. At the start of June 2021, the figure had increased to 419 and has been growing at 3 parts per million every year. The amount of carbon dioxide in the atmosphere is now much higher than it has been for the past one million years, which scientists can measure by looking at tiny bubbles of ice trapped in the Antarctic ice sheet.[20]

We've noticed the effect this is having. Back in the 1990s, scientists were telling us that if we kept on increasing the amount of greenhouse gases, then through the 21st century the Earth would get warmer. The past ten years have been the warmest decade since we started measuring global temperature 150 years ago. Already, on average, the Earth is one degree warmer than it was back then. And as the Earth gets warmer, the weather gets wilder. We are seeing weather patterns begin to change, including:

- Stronger hurricanes in the tropics due to warmer seas
- More intense rainstorms and flooding
- Intense heat waves and droughts which affect people and all life
- Melting glaciers all over the world, which also leads to flooding and rising sea levels
- Melting and thinning ice sheets over the North Pole.

People, plants and animals are already beginning to be affected by these changes. Many animals are finding that their habitats are changing at a rate faster than they can adapt to, leading sadly to some becoming extinct. Scientists estimate that the rate of extinction is ten times higher than should be occurring naturally.

Now, the biggest effects of climate change are being felt in places where the poorest people live. For example, in the Pacific, people who live on small islands are being flooded out of their homes and farms due to sea level rise and stronger storms. The sad thing is that being poor, these people have only added a little carbon dioxide in to the atmosphere as they do not use much electricity or fossil fuels. It's the rich and developed nations that have contributed most to climate change, yet we do not feel its impacts greatly now.

But if we continue to use fossil fuels at the same rate as we have been doing, then our climate models predict that the Earth will become another four degrees warmer than it is now and we will all notice its effects upon our lives. The effects upon weather, sea levels, ice caps and on people, plants and animals will be much more extreme than we are seeing now, affecting all our lives across the planet as well as all the other animals and plants that are part of the creation that God loves and says is good.[21]

Becoming wild

Using their climate models, scientists tell us that we need keep the warming of the planet due to increasing greenhouse gases to between one-and-a-half and two degrees centigrade. To do this, we need to care more about the atmosphere, reducing the amount of carbon dioxide we add to zero by 2050 at the latest. So, what can we each do to make a difference?

God asks us to care for the Earth. The story of the first people in the Bible says, 'The Lord God took [them] and put [them] in the garden of Eden to work it and take care of it' (Genesis 2:15). Yet climate change seems such a big issue. What might we each do to make a difference to protect people and all creatures now and in the future? How can we care for our atmosphere?

A few years ago, I visited Peru to spend time with Christians working on caring for the environment in the Amazon jungle.[22] As we went along the Amazon River one day in a small wooden boat, I noticed some beautiful butterflies feeding on fruit on the banks of the river – all different vibrant colours – greens, blues, yellows. They reminded me of a story told in science called the 'the butterfly effect'. It explains something of how the weather works. Imagine one of those butterflies flapping its wings on the banks of the Amazon. Can you imagine how small a puff of wind that might make? Almost too small to feel or even measure. But, from that small waft of wind, it could be that five days later over the other side of the world, a huge storm will develop with winds so strong they will blow you and buildings over!

In the atmosphere, small things matter. And in our living, small things can make a big difference too. That is what Jesus' story of the mustard seed in the Bible tells us. It's how God works in our lives and in the world, sharing and shaping things by his life – often not in big ways or through 'important' people. Just look at how Messy Church has grown from a single community to thousands all over the world over the past 15 years!

So what small things can we do to make a difference? Here are a few suggestions as to how we can take care of our atmosphere and lessen the impact of climate change by reducing the amount of greenhouse gases that we make in our ordinary everyday lives, and amazingly extraordinary Messy Churches.

1 **Get wild** – Get outdoors! Take some time to look up at the wonder of creation. The more we appreciate God's creation, the more we will have the heart to care for it and not damage it. Look around you at the plants and trees. Watch out for wild animals and birds – and don't forget the butterflies! Look up and watch the wonder of the clouds, changing each day. Plant a tree or some plants as a sign that you want to help reduce the amount of carbon dioxide in the atmosphere. And as you look, what do the things you see tell you about God and how he cares for us and all that he has made?

2 **Get wise** – Think about how you use energy. Make sure you switch off lights and heating in your homes and buildings where you meet for Messy Church when you don't need them on. Check where the electricity for the buildings comes from. Is the supplier using renewable wind, solar or hydroelectric power to supply your electricity? Ask your church leaders about it. You can find out how

much carbon dioxide your activities produce with the Climate Stewards Carbon Calculator.[23]

3 **Get local** – Think about the food you buy and use in your Messy Church. Where has it come from: locally, or has it travelled around the world releasing a lot of carbon dioxide? Look up how much carbon dioxide and other greenhouse gases producing different foods makes. Producing meat often releases more of the gases that cause the Earth to warm than growing vegetables. Could you reduce the amount of meat in your diet and Messy Church meals?

4 **Get walking** – How do you travel to Messy Church? How do you travel to school? Could you walk rather than go in the car? Might you need to change the way your Messy Church is run to allow people more time to get to it? Does your building provide places people can store their bikes and scooters safely?

5 **Get informed** – Look out for stories in the media and on the internet for how our climate is changing. Find out about how climate change and wilder weather is affecting people around the Earth. Could you write as a Messy Church to your MP about your concerns about climate change and ask the government to work with other countries to reduce its impact upon our lives and poor people around the world? Why not send them some pictures from your Messy Church that show how special God's world is?

Five small things will make a huge difference: a difference to *our* world now, giving hope to those people who are part of our worldwide Messy Church family who are already struggling with climate change, and a difference to *the* world. Our actions may allow people to continue to enjoy the wonder of creation, and through it come to appreciate the wonder of the creator.

6

Caring for all God's Messy people

Crystal Goetz

Crystal Goetz loves Messy Church! Her involvement as an ambassador and trainer for Messy Church USA and director of her local Messy Church in Auburn, Washington, are only a few ways that she hopes to inspire others with her love of Jesus and her passion for Messy Church.

See the need

Messy Church is a special place. When I think of Messy Church, I think of community and common ground, because Messy Church is a worship experience that includes everyone. Through the five values of all-age, celebration, hospitality, creativity and Christ-centredness, we gather together with commonality. We form a bond that unites us in purpose and an unspoken sense of responsibility for each other. That's how Messy Church works: together we are better. Together we care.

When we speak of being God's Messy people, we must carefully define what the word 'messy' means. In our context, it means that life is complicated and so are we. That what we experience in our lives is a roller-coaster ride of highs and lows that sometimes look so complicated that we might well call them messy. Through this messiness, God shows us love and care and asks us to respond to each other in kindness. Caring for all of God's Messy people is an important component of any Messy Church. In our gatherings, the greater good becomes a part of the plan and we begin a process of learning to make choices that are for the good of all. When leading or participating in Messy Church, community is a conscious effort and requires a bit of work, a smidgeon of patience and a pinch of compassion.

What constitutes caring for God's Messy people? That's a huge question and one that doesn't necessarily come to mind when we are busily preparing for our Messy congregations to dance through our doors. However, it is vital in bringing a Messy Church to people, that is, truly sharing the message that Jesus brought to the people – love God, love your neighbour, love yourself. But where do we start? Who are the vulnerable ones that we want to look out for? Also, in caring for others, are we still caring for our world and for ourselves?

The questions are dizzying, and in order to find the answer we need to jump down Alice's rabbit hole. When we begin to ponder, it leaves us feeling as if we might not ever get to the actual doing of Messy Church because we are too busy planning. There is also a potential for paradoxes. In helping one group of people, we could potentially harm another. When one considers all the possibilities, it seems preferable to throw up your hands and not even try. Think about it like a tangled ball of string. Just when you think it will never be untangled, and you have been trying to free the knots for hours, you pull one string in just the right way and it's ready to use. It's time to pull on that string together.

Let's begin with this: when we talk about caring for God's Messy people, it's helpful to define who God's Messy people are. This is an easy one. They are all of us. Each and every soul is messy and precious to God. Each life: beautiful and perfect in cherished messiness. When people are not allowed to be their divine messy selves due to poverty, exclusion, persecution or lack of resources, the world suffers for it. Jesus calls for us to love our neighbours and tells us who we should be as neighbours and who our neighbours are. It is a responsibility that Jesus left us to tend to. You might be saying, 'I am just a little Messy Church. I don't know if I can take that on.' I know it seems like a huge task, but God intends us to be good stewards of our world and that includes the people who inhabit it. This is where it gets very Messy, but we are on a journey together, so stick with me. Here is an example of what I mean.

In my local community there is a long-term care facility. It not only houses those who come for a short stay, recovering from surgery or a serious illness, but long-term residents who, day after day, look out of the tiny windows of their rooms into a parking lot. There is a distinct lack of joy that permeates the walls of that place. Each year, our church gives the long-term residents Christmas gifts. We ask each person to write down two things they need and one thing they want. Never in the ten years we have provided those gifts have we ever had an extravagant request. Most of the time, what the residents want are things like a case of soda 'all their own' or some nice-smelling hand lotion. Most of the things that they need are socks, blankets and sweatpants.

When we realised what conditions were like there, we asked if we could come in and do Messy Vintage (see messychurch.org.uk/messy-vintage), a programme designed for older people, with them. Immediately the activities director said, 'Yes, please', and we held the event as soon as we could schedule it. While it was chaotic and one of our volunteers was a little overwhelmed, it was a beautiful thing to see the joy in people's faces doing a craft that was new and different. Having conversations and getting to know a little about them made us all realise that these people were just like us, just experiencing different circumstances. That Messy experience was day-altering for them, but also for us. By observing a need and making a simple plan, we were able to care for those people in such a simple way.

That was just helping out in our small town, one tiny thing. We also need to look beyond our communities and begin to see the tightly woven web of how our lives, work and ministries are connected to those in other areas – whether that community is people who look or speak differently from us, or whose belief systems are not like ours, or who cannot do things for themselves without some extra care from those able to help them. We are all interdependent. Together we are better. Together we care.

Be the change

Church is a method of caring for God's people in a very intangible way. It could be said that by the mere presence of a Messy Church congregation in your church you are showing great care for God's people. Let me explain. There are many ways to hear the gospel and many ways to tell it. There really is no better way to experience it than in a Messy Church setting. From the moment you walk through the door, it's all about welcome and hospitality. This is an expression of God's kingdom, a place where everyone is welcome. As God's beloved people learning through and demonstrating activities and using creativity, we experience the love of Jesus, and we learn those big lessons: God loves us; God wants good things for us; God is with us. Whether you experience it sitting across from someone who has autism or someone with white hair, it's all about caring for each other every time. Being present and touching the lives of those around you is one great way to care for God's Messy people!

Our modern world has quite suddenly thrown people who were thousands of miles apart into the mix together. Via Zoom or on social media, we communicate daily with people all over the world. This is one of the messiest places and where there is a real need to help God's Messy people. It may not seem like an issue to those who have developed a partnership with the cyber world and with technology. However, there are quite a few people who resist technology and its implications. Here we see a need and we have a way to fill it. Those who have gifts involving technology have the ability to show others how it can help us in our ministries.

The use of technology in Messy Church is not a new thing. We have all had to rely on it – in these last years, a great deal – and it has woken us up to the fact that we can reach out beyond the walls of our church building in new and inventive ways. Online Messy Church sessions, virtual planning meetings, searching for ideas on our favourite websites are all ways that we use technology in our Messy Churches. At the same time, it is a cautionary tale. There are places in the world where mining practices for some of the elements in our laptops and mobile phones are not only bad for the planet but create health and welfare issues for those who actually mine those elements. There are many news stories that highlight the work we have to do in the area of producing technology, but by reaching out to those who are technologically challenged there is a great opportunity to share our God-given gifts and instruct others.

We use technology for communication and words matter. Through our language and the words we use, we can also care for others. It is difficult to get our heads around the use of our modern language sometimes. There are new words, phrases and expressions being used and invented, it seems, every day. What about the times when language can be a barrier to inclusion? We can care when we use our various languages carefully and take the time to make sure that people who are multilingual are being served and helping in our Messy Churches. Let's see an example.

Hector and his family walk into your Messy Church. The children are bilingual Spanish and English speakers, but Hector only speaks Spanish. His daughter, Jessenya, 13, is the caregiver of her younger siblings that range in age from three to eleven. Their mother is working on the night of Messy Church and can't attend with the family. Jessenya is overwhelmed after a long day of school and tired when she walks through the door. Hector speaks to her calmly and quietly. She nods and turns to you at the welcome table.

Jessenya clearly is familiar with being the interpreter in a situation like this and is ready to communicate with you, when you notice that the other three children are running around in the activity space that you are using for Messy Church. They squeal with delight at all of the things they see.

Let's stop this scenario for a moment and see it from a caring perspective. What is needed here? A broom and dustpan? A firm hand and harsh words? How about this: quick thinking and a generous supply of love, compassion and inclusivity?

Let's continue our story. You quickly ask Jessenya if she has another sibling who can interpret for her father. Then you ask her to have the kids take a seat and have a snack with her. You invite a table host to help them figure out what to do next. Meanwhile, that extra sibling can help fill out paperwork while Jessenya gets a much-needed break. It would also be handy to know if there is anyone on your team who is multilingual and use those gifts to the advantage of your welcome table.

Especially in European communities, being multilingual is quite common. A 2012 EU study cites that 54% of Europeans can hold a conversation in at least one other language. If you have a Messy Church team that comprises ten people, approximately five of them might be, at least, bilingual and perhaps multilingual. What a great gift. In the US, the numbers are staggeringly less. Only 20% can converse in at least one other language, according to the 2020 Census Bureau statistics. This is challenging, but not insurmountable. With great tools like language apps for your phone (there's that pesky technology again), you can learn to communicate. Find out how to say, 'Do you need assistance in communicating? We have a person who speaks [insert language here], who can help you.' Then page that helper and, voilà, instant friends. That's how Messy Church works: together we are better. Together we care.

Language isn't the only barrier to caring for God's Messy people. There is also difficulty for people with disabilities, including mental illness. How do we show the value of hospitality to those Messy people?

Treating each other with a genuine sense of value is important to all people. Each person, even those who may require extra attention, want to feel that they have a purpose and can contribute in some way.

In our local Messy Church, we have a woman who is diagnosed as having several mental illnesses as well as cognitive challenges. One Messy Church session she began to argue with me about a project – ecobricks, to be exact. I was explaining to her that since we can't do anything about the plastic waste that is already in our environment, people around the world are using them as construction materials. I explained that the plastic waste was polluting our beaches and oceans and that animals were being harmed as a result. At first, she argued and didn't understand, to the point of frustration on all sides, but patiently we forged ahead in our conversation. Then you could see, the moment that she understood she stopped arguing and started smiling. It had now become part of her world. She spent the rest of the evening resolutely shoving plastic into a two-litre bottle with a piece of wooden dowel and was so happy, because at last, she had a purpose. She was going to rid the world of plastic, one piece at a time. She has since brought us more than 40 ecobricks and has a lot of pride in the fact that she is helping. It would have been very easy to get frustrated and dismiss her as someone to be avoided in the future. Instead, we lavished time and attention on her, and she found a place where she could feel like she mattered and had value.

It is in the same way that we can find ways to welcome and include those who would otherwise be marginalised in our Messy Churches. Learn to use pronouns on your nametags and more gender-neutral language when talking about the Bible to be more welcoming of those in the LGBTQIA+ community. In doing this one small thing, you are showing that you care for all God's people.

Also, we sometimes think that physical touch can calm someone, but in the case of people on the autism spectrum, human touch is not welcomed; in fact, it can cause a very negative reaction. Sometimes technology can help to lower social anxiety for people on the autism spectrum. Through some trial and error, we've discovered technology can be just what is needed to be inclusive and caring in our Messy Churches for this particular group. Having a touch screen with an interactive game or trivia about Jesus or the theme at your Messy Church session can help.

Going touchless and speechless can have a great impact. I have found much personal enjoyment interacting with a local man who is on the autism spectrum by building a figure with interlocking bricks or tangram shapes. Not a word was spoken, but much was communicated with the shapes that we built together. Think about how to make everyone's experience at Messy Church a personal 'Hallelujah'! Together we are better. Together we care.

Extend our reach

One of the areas where there can be a cauldron of confusion is sourcing your supplies for Messy Church. Are they environmentally friendly? How are they sourced? Are the people who are making the items cared for properly in the job? We can care about Messy people by providing opportunities to support their families and make their lives easier by taking a little time to answer these questions. Why should we care, you ask? We should care because that is how we make change and that is what Jesus would do. That is how we help lift people up and help them to have the life that God wants for them.

Some things to consider when purchasing supplies or food:

- Are you purchasing your items from a company that supports workers and consumers?
- Is there a choice offered where you could support a minority-owned or small business?
- Is there a Fairtrade, responsibly sourced option?
- Is the country of origin of your product offering union workshops and workers' rights?

- Is there a way to drive the larger share businesses to help the smaller vulnerable businesses through website promotion or in other ways?

I know what you are thinking: 'SHEESH! Too much! I just want to make a pot of coffee!' Consider this: if we ask these questions when operating our Messy Churches, what kind of changes will we begin to see? If we care, truly care, for all God's Messy people, then we have to ask these questions. When we do, we begin to see the big picture of God's wonderful dream for our world – one that lets everyone live the best life that they possibly can.

We need to search for the oppressed and seek out opportunities to help. Even the smallest thing can be an improvement for them and for your Messy Church. Figuring out a new way to do something can lead to great things. If we start our process of caring with ourselves and work outward, our reach is vast. Echoing through the world, beginning with a whisper and ending in a shout. A pebble thrown into a lake makes many ripples. So can we, in how we operate in Messy Church.

Interestingly, in the ripple effect, each of the concentric circles encompasses the circle that came before and on and on, seemingly forever. That is how our ministry must work with our world if we wish to truly care for others. We should ask an important question: who is at the centre of the circles? Where does it all start? Does it start with us, our church, our suppliers or just our neighbour in conversation? The answer is so simple. I think you must know the answer even before it is revealed. Jesus, of course. Jesus was the perfect example of how to care for others. Just like Jesus, it's important that we take care in everything we do; that we care for the people we are in direct contact with, but also the person across the world in the factory who makes the supplies we use in Messy Church. When is a good time to start caring? Right now. Together we are better. Together we care.

Five things you can do now to care for God's Messy people

1 Pay attention to what you buy and where you buy your Messy Church food and supplies, and try to use the source that has the best impact on people and the environment.

2 Do some research about places and companies that pay their workers a living wage and provide healthy, dignified working conditions.

3 Include anyone and everyone in your Messy Church. Show them they are valued. Find a place for everyone.

4 Recruit extra help to work with Messy people in your Messy Church to help them feel included. Messy buddies would be a help for some who struggle to navigate in the Messy Church environment.

5 Pray for the Messy Churches of the world to show care in all they do to help all of God's Messy people. A great way to connect with the worldwide wonderful network of Messy Churches!

7

And a little child shall lead them...

Rachel Summers

Rachel Summers is a forest school practitioner and trainer based in East London, alongside training as an ordained pioneer minister with the Church of England. She loves helping people to rediscover their urban wild spaces, has plenty of good ideas (some of which actually happen) and her hands are never quite mud free.

Anyone who has ever tried to walk anywhere with a tiny toddler will well know how very long it takes. It's not just that they walk slowly, thanks to their little legs, but that they notice *everything*. Maybe that's because they're shorter and closer to the ground. Maybe it's that they creep along at a snail's pace. But maybe it's because they haven't yet taught themselves that the world is ordinary and commonplace and somewhere to be travelled through on the way to somewhere else.

So often when we are trying to craft opportunities for worship, for prayer, for unpacking the things of God, we come in the role of the expert. After all, we know the Bible readings, perhaps we've read some stuff about it or heard sermons on the subject, and our skill that comes in here is of finding the nubbin of the message and creating a parcel that can be unpacked by people of all ages, children and toddlers included, allowing them to hear the message in a way they will understand. This is valuable, joyful work, and how wonderful it is to see the myriad creative ways in which this takes place. But what if we allowed these tiny ones to teach us what we've forgotten – the truth that this world is an intricate and astounding place of wonder, a precious creation that shows us our creator?

Often when I speak of prayer to people who don't have an experience of prayer themselves, I talk of it as 'noticing'. Noticing my body breathing, the ground my feet are touching, the way the leaves are moving above my hammock. All of this feels like prayer to me, as it's all part of how I plunge into that awareness that I am held in the love of something and someone far bigger than I can properly grasp. Noticing the world around me helps me to feel deep within my very bones my connection with everything else in creation, and in turn with the creator who made and loves us all.

Spending time outside in nature with children is an exercise in noticing. If we have the courage to hold back from our adult impulse to point out, to name and explain, to drive the experience ourselves, we will, if we are blessed, be welcomed in as guests into the child's world and a child's-eye-view of creation. We will crouch beside a rock, sun-warmed, and turn it over to find a family of woodlice revealed, as exciting as a Christmas stocking. As we sit by the ash tree, we will watch the ants on their trail up and down the trunk, harvesting the sticky honeydew from their aphid livestock. We can watch as a stick is drawn through the mud and creates a line, that then oozily refills itself.

We begin to find that we have slowed ourselves down. That as we catch the awe of each tiny, commonplace thing, we begin to glimpse something of the vastness of God. We begin to understand ourselves as tiny, commonplace things, caught up in the vastness of the created universe, and yet know ourselves to be precious, just as these things are precious. And as we do so, we begin to learn alongside the children what God has to show us through the world he created us to be a part of. Perhaps watching the woodlice will speak to us of the loving parenting of God, as we notice the tiny baby woodlice clinging on to their mama's underbelly. Maybe as we watch the ants farming their aphids with love and care, we will be struck by a reflection of God's love and care even in these tiny creatures. As we play in the mud, we might ponder our sinful marks upon the world and how complete God's forgiveness is.

In Play Theory, that state where a child is so engrossed in their play and have sunk so deeply into it that they are oblivious to the world around is called Flow. It is in Flow state that all the good stuff happens. Academic learning, for sure, understanding narrative, volume and changing states of matter – but also learning those soft skills of perseverance, courageous experimentation and flexibility of thought, all held in deep, satisfying joy. In Flow state, one is secure enough to take risks. It is not a coincidence, I feel, that when a new worshipping community was discipled among a group of young skateboarders, they discussed the name of God – and Flow was what emerged. Certainly, a state of Flow seems very similar to a state of prayer, to me, a thin place, where we are able to listen and to take things in in an undefended way. A place where we can learn and grow, experiment and take risks in our faith, and be held in deep, satisfying joy.

Being outside, with its limitless supply of creative opportunity, easily nudges children into this state. I expect it does the same to us, if we are brave enough to let it. Playing with toys puts too much already-decided expectation into the pot. A doll can only be a doll; a fire engine only a fire engine. Yet how many things can a stick be? There's a fantastic picture book called *Stanley's Stick*, where his stick is a whistle, a rocket, a spoon, and a dinosaur.[24] Playing around with and among the things of nature is very freeing. Being outdoors literally takes the lid off our learning and exploring. Rather than being constrained by what we have already decided to put inside a place, we are gifted this openness where there is enough and more than enough. Margaret MacMillan, a visionary figure in the world of nursery education in the early 20th century, wrote that 'the best classroom and the richest cupboard are roofed only by the sky'. What a place for our loving God to put us to learn.

I think that sometimes we feel that to get the best out of nature, we need to access it in a particular way or a particular place. The government or local council helpfully demarcates some green spaces as 'Areas of Outstanding Natural Beauty', National Parks or nature reserves. This can be a useful pointer – how magical to walk somewhere where every step you might stumble upon something wonderful and rare. Sometimes, like a pilgrimage, it can be good to journey somewhere special, to surround ourselves with the soil, plants and wildlife of a particular environment. Stepping into a place where we are expecting to meet with precious surprises means that we are more likely to notice them and appreciate them fully.

There's an equality of opportunities thing here, isn't there? Some of us may live within national parks. Some of us may have the money, the leisure time and the confidence to travel to such places even if we live farther away. And yet, what we know of God is that what God offers is offered to all. Perhaps God is coaxing us to begin to explore the wild places right on our doorstep.

You may be thinking that you have no wild places near to where you live. Put on your wild spectacles and look again. Is there a piece of waste ground beside the building site? I know people who have found rare bee-orchids in a place like this. What about a tidy churchyard? If you worked with the community to unpack the benefits of leaving at least some of it to rewild, you would be knee-deep in meadow grasses within a couple of seasons, wading through it like the sea as cinnabar moths flutter out from the grass breakers. Even as you stride along the street towards the shop, you might begin to notice the hawkbit bursting golden through the cracks at the edge of the pavement.

After all, God has a habit of delighting in the beauty of the unloved and forgotten. Isaiah writes, 'Break forth into joy, sing together, ye waste places of Jerusalem' (Isaiah 52:9, KJV), and I have found great joy when beauty has been revealed to me in waste places. The younger son; the smallest family; the inconsequential and unimportant – all these are the vehicles through which God is able to show his love and saving power. Choosing to spend our time in these forgotten places may well mean that we are somewhere God may playfully speak to us through the world she has created.

Sometimes people worry that worshipping outdoors may mean people are unclear about the place of Jesus, feeling uncomfortably as though they may be edging into the realms of paganism or new-age spirituality. And it is true that for many people outside the church, nature is a place where they find some sense of spiritual connection. We have seen this so strongly over the past couple of years, as over lockdown people craved access to their local green spaces. Neighbourhoods filled with people looking at and appreciating their local street trees, pocket parks and playing fields as never before – places they always knew were there but had seldom visited, always passing them by on the way to someplace else. But throughout history Christians have always connected to God and Jesus through the natural world.

In a time of uncertainty, people long to feel part of something greater than themselves, to see the hope of life continuing instead of the round of endless fear on the media. Watching the seasons turn and knowing that summer would follow spring, and autumn follow summer, brought people peace and reminded them of their place in the universe. Our human busyness can blind us to the fact that we are nevertheless simply part of nature, being pulled along for the ride. What a gift we as the church can offer to people, walking alongside them as they seek meaning in the greening of the trees and the drawing in of the nights. Not only do we know who created all of this, and us as part of it, but we *know* them ourselves. How fantastic to be able to share a mutual love for nature with those around us, and to hold their hand as they search for the connection they can feel tugging at them through the wonders around them. As it says in Romans 1:20 (NRSV), 'Ever since the creation of the world his eternal power and divine nature, invisible though they are, have been understood and seen through the things he has made.' Our times, as technologically extraordinary as they are, are no exception.

Increasingly, families, children and young people are getting involved in climate activism. In Tearfund's survey 'Burning Down the House', they discovered that 9 out of 10 young people were concerned about the climate crisis, but only 1 out of 10 believed their church was doing enough about it. Connecting with nature is a very simple first step towards climate activism. After all, you only want to save something you know, and you only get to know something by spending time with it. In a study from 2016, it was found that three-quarters of children spend less time outside than prison inmates. Providing children and families with an opportunity to access nature feels like a missional activity, not only for their physical and mental health, but for their spiritual health too. Engaging with children and families on an issue that they care passionately about means that we have a point at which we connect, and as the church we have so much we can bring to the table – our understanding of the world being a gift, of us being placed here to care for it and not to exploit it, of a sense of hope even in the middle of despair.

So much then for the reasons why we should support children and families to access nature in order that they might discover God there. But what about the day we have a session scheduled, activities planned, and the heavens open and it pours with rain? How do we do all of this good stuff when we live on a planet that has weather? I expect you have heard the old adage that there is no such thing as bad weather, only bad clothing. It's true that having the right things to wear makes all the difference – sun hat in bright weather, full waterproofs (including waterproof trousers) in the rain. If we want children and families to relax into God's love through his creation, they will need to be comfortable, and part of that is being warm and dry. We mustn't assume that people instinctively know how to do this. Often the outdoors is somewhere to be passed through on the way to something else, and so spending an extended period outside means people may need to have it really clearly explained to them how to dress to be comfortable. Not everyone will own the right kit – maybe as a church community we can be part of that solution, sourcing wellies and waterproofs and providing them as necessary.

The advantage of having weather, of course, is that it is part of God's creation and has plenty to teach us and for us to explore within it. We understand God as our shelter on a much deeper emotional level after huddling under a shelter with our family and friends as the rain pours down upon us, cascading off the edges and splashing on the floor. How are we to understand the Holy Spirit as a rushing wind if we haven't felt that air pushing against us on a windy day, tugging at our kite string, filling our jackets as we unzip them and hold them out as we run against it? We begin to understand hope as something real and concrete when we look at twigs on a dark, foggy winter's day and notice that they already hold the tightly coiled-up buds of spring.

Taking opportunities for worship outside also takes some courage. After all, the indoors is safe and predictable. Outdoors there is risk – stinging nettles, branches to trip over, mud to slip up on. But faith itself is a risky business. Jesus never said that following him would make our life safe; in fact, quite the opposite. Exploring faith while we also explore risk feels to me to be a good place to do it. When I teach forest school trainees about risk assessment, I get them to write a third column – not just the column for the risk and the action they will take to minimise this risk, but a column marked 'risk benefit'. That's the magic bit, the 'why on earth are we doing this risky activity' bit. You will find that once you start thinking of those outdoors risks in terms of the benefits they offer, not only just for fun or learning, but spiritual benefits, then it becomes instantly clear how wonderful being outside will be for your families and children.

Take a slippery, muddy path, for example. The risk is obvious – someone might slip and hurt themselves. Maybe your action will be that all children will walk this path holding the hand of an adult. But the risk benefit? I'm thinking of that bit in the Psalms, 'He lifted me out of the slimy pit, out of the mud and mire' (Psalm 40:2). Knowing that your feet are slipping, being scared that you will fall in the mud and knowing that someone you love and trust will pull you to safety? What a brilliant way for God's loving care for us to be made visible.

The more we practise, the more we see God's loving care made visible to us through nature, through her creation. As children and families feel that sense of freedom outside, they will be discovering the freedom that God has gifted us all. As they crouch down, quietly watching the world around them, they will touch upon God's peace. As they shriek with muddy joy, they will be filled with God's joy. And as we all grow in love for our planet, we will know ourselves too to be loved beyond measure.

PART II

MESSY RESPONSES

8

Around the world the Messy way

What international Messy Church leaders are concerned about and how they encourage their Messy Churches to take action

Australia

Sandy Brodine

Sandy Brodine is a minister in the Uniting Church in Australia with a passion for finding creative new ways to help people follow Jesus and engage with their faith. Sandy ministers with a number of new faith communities in the Banyule Network of Uniting Churches: a Messy Church, an intergenerational interactive Sunday community called Common Ground, and SPACE, a contemplative community. Prior to ministry, Sandy was a teacher of Chinese, English and RE in secondary school. Sandy is married to Brendan, and they have a daughter Sophia. In her free time, Sandy enjoys fibre arts, painting icons, genealogy, cooking and travel.

Australia is a vast country with wide and varied landscapes and climates. While it is a country of great beauty, our land is also a dangerous place to live, where summer can see one part of the country ravaged by bushfire and another under dangerous flooding. It is not surprising, therefore, that concern about climate emergency is strong.

Within our churches, we also have a growing understanding that issues of climate and care for the environment cannot be separated from our relationships with our indigenous brothers and sisters, and their knowledge of and love for this land. 'Country': the relationship to the land of their ancestors is the fundamental basis of life for Australian indigenous peoples.[25]

Although the indigenous peoples have cared for the land, we 'second peoples' who arrived as colonisers have done much damage both to the land and to our relationships with those who were here before us. These issues are complex and painful and are ones that we are only beginning to wrestle with.

As a beginning step to acknowledging this reality of our situation, the Uniting Church in Australia recognises this in the Preamble to the Constitution:

> Through this land God had nurtured and sustained the First Peoples of this country, the Aboriginal and Islander peoples, who continue to understand themselves to be the traditional owners and custodians (meaning 'sovereign' in the languages of the First Peoples) of these lands and waters since time immemorial.[26]

Not only are our indigenous people the custodians of the land, but they are the holders of the local creation stories, which show that country is more than just a dwelling place for human beings:

> It is also the place in which the creator-ancestors live and continue to speak and guide through river, mountain, sea and myriad animals and plants. The land is… something of a sacred

text for Indigenous peoples. Properly read and understood, it shows us who we are and what we are to do in this world.[27]

We are learning to walk alongside our indigenous sisters and brothers as second peoples in this land, and to learn from them about how to care for this land, as they had done for millennia before our arrival.

It is hardly surprising, then, that a theology that understands God as creator and sustainer, and one that invites us into relationship with one another and the care of God's creation alongside God, permeates our Messy Churches. At the simplest level, many Messy Churches have begun using sustainable or natural materials for activities, rather than plastic, glitter or other environmentally damaging materials.

We are beginning to grow and develop our understanding of how God calls us to care for the environment and reconcile with one another into our Messy Church programmes, so that our Messy Church communities can embody the kind of love that the Triune God lavishes upon us. The hospitality and invitation to reconciliation that God has shown us form practices that we share with one another as we gather around scripture and wrestle with it Messily, when we celebrate what God has done with us, and for us, and as we eat together in shared community.

Here are two ways we have sought to engage with environmental issues in our intergenerational churches locally in the last 18 months:

1 **'Make a Difference' (MAD) project** – Led by our youth, we spent a month or so exploring ways that we could make a difference to the world around us during worship. The teens decided that we should do a clean-up project in our local park, and so armed with tongs and garbage bags we spent a very cold Sunday morning picking up rubbish in the local park as our worship. The group also got very involved in making ecobricks. It is remarkable how much time it took to make one brick, and how many people were involved. Everyone was amazed at how much soft plastic can be sequestered away in just one 1.25 litre bottle!

2 **Messy Science** – We have an annual Messy Church event that is focused on God's creation and the environment. The scientists who are part of preparing each session see themselves as working alongside a God who is continuously active in creation, to find ways to help create solutions to environmental problems. We looked at compost and how long it takes various things to break down, and did some experiments. Everyone was fascinated by a Melbourne University science award-winning innovation – the 'Urinotron', which makes enough power to run a mobile phone out of body waste![28]

Moving forward, I hope that we can continue to plan to intentionally implant this theological perspective into all we do in Messy Church, so that we can listen to, and learn more intentionally from, our indigenous brothers and sisters, who have so much to teach us about how to care for our planet, and with whom we seek to be reconciled.

Canada

Carol Fletcher and Mark Hird-Rutter

Carol Fletcher lives out her faith through a passion for welcoming people into inclusive community. Involved in Messy Church since 2011, Carol became team lead for Messy Church Canada in 2021. Carol serves in team ministry with spouse Jeff Cook at Winnipeg's Transcona Memorial – part of The United Church of Canada.

Mark Hird-Rutter has been a regional coordinator for Messy Church in British Columbia, Canada. Now retired, he has been working as a Messy Church leader since 2009.

Caring for creation must include thinking about water and how we care for it. In Genesis, the story of creation begins with the Spirit of God hovering over the face of the waters. The Assembly of First Nations of Canada says: 'Water is the most life sustaining gift on Mother Earth and is the interconnection among all living beings.'[29] We need to learn from our own faith history and indigenous wisdom.

It's a Messy world. And Canada is a wild and Messy place!

Being environmentally friendly is an important part of living with respect in creation. We are called to care for one another and all the earth, to be good stewards of creation: people, animals, land, air and water.

Canada has a relatively small population for a very big country. As of 2021, there are about 38 million people in almost 10 million square kilometres! With a big and diverse land that includes majestic mountains, vast prairies, beautiful lakes, exquisite Arctic and solid rocks, it is easy for us to see the beauty of the earth. And, even with all this, it is also easy for us to see the fragility of creation and the impact of human living – whether it be careless litter or large-scale pollution that contributes to climate change.

Messy Church has the ability to gather people around the ideas of caring for creation in small-scale projects that have a big impact, for example 'Grow a Row' for a local food bank. And Messy Church has the ability to help form further thinking that can have larger impacts as people make creation-sensitive choices. Telling our stories is sharing our faith.

In Canada there is lots of concern about water. Canada extends from coast to coast to coast (there are coastlines on the Atlantic, the Pacific and the Arctic oceans). We have more than 2 million lakes and rivers. In the mountains in Western Canada there are many glaciers and ice sheets. These glaciers feed great rivers that flow north, east, south and west. We cannot imagine what will happen when all the glaciers melt!

At the moment, there is a lot of water, but the quality of the water is highly impacted by how we treat it and how we treat all of the lands that touch it.

And, when we have made mistakes, we can work with nature to bring healing. For example, many years ago, Britannia Beach silver-copper mine was on Howe Sound in British Columbia. For decades after the mine was closed, pollutants from the mine leached into the river and ocean. Nothing lived in the river from the mine to about one kilometre into the ocean from the mouth of the river. When the British Columbia government decided to clean up the river, they built a dam on it with a filter system. The dam generated electricity, which fed back to the grid. The filters took out all the pollutants and these could be refined into copper and silver. They made enough to pay for the cost of the facility. The miracle was that in 18 months, salmon swam in the river again for the first time in 100 years. Given a chance, nature can do so much.

But we must help. In Messy Church we often connect with one another and with our faith through crafts. In doing this, we must pay close attention to what story we are telling, what we are using to tell that story and why we are using it. We should seek to avoid non-biodegradable garbage that ends up in water – blowing in from landfills, litter or the like. Messy Church activities that reduce plastics and garbage are so important. Activities that start with 'reuse and recycle' can help us to 'reduce', can help us to develop our own creativity and can allow others to use their imaginations in celebrating faith.

At Messy Church, water is used for everything from drinking and washing hands to crafts and experiments. Every connection with water can be a learning point about water usage and about respect. Messy Science can connect people to local wildlife or nature facilities, demonstrate water filters, teach us about phosphates and encourage us to commit to environmentally friendly soaps in our Messy Church and in our homes.

Understanding and caring for water can be a part of the Canadian and global journey of relationship and reconciliation with first peoples and with nature. We continue to work and to learn together as we acknowledge, again and again, the complexities of life together.

Germany

Damaris Binder

 Damaris Binder is a regional coordinator for Germany, where Messy Church is called Kirche Kunterbunt. She has been part of creating regional hubs across Germany, offering people a Messy Church contact person in their region.

In Germany we're observing a fast-growing awareness for a sustainable ecological lifestyle within society – due to, among other factors, the Fridays For Future movement. This development also shows in the little things, not least that the interest for outdoor Messy Church activities is increasing immensely and that many people wish to live more sustainably, more consciously and closer to nature.

As Kirche Kunterbunt (literally 'colourful church', the German Messy Church), we want to take God's mandate to preserve the creation seriously. Therefore, we put a special emphasis on handling resources in a responsible way. In practice, this means that we urge the Kirche Kunterbunt groups to produce as little waste as possible and to avoid activity stations in which they use food items that have to be thrown away after use. It is our concern as Kirche Kunterbunt to make people love God's creation and to sensitise them to God's mandate to preserve it.

To this end, we developed a session outline which the Kirche Kunterbunt groups can implement locally. Its focus is how we can fulfil God's mandate to preserve the creation a little better.

Holy in love with God's world

Aim

The topic 'Holy in love with God's world' should put our love for this earth into focus. We want to sensitise people to the topic of sustainability. God gave us a mandate to preserve his creation, and what this means and how we can fulfil it a little better are the central questions of this session.

Bible link

> So God created mankind in his own image, in the image of God he created them; male and female he created them.
>
> God blessed them and said to them, 'Be fruitful and increase in number; fill the earth and subdue it. Rule over the fish in the sea and the birds in the sky and over every living creature that moves on the ground.'
>
> GENESIS 1:27–28

The story of creation, specifically the two verses from Genesis 1:27–28, shows clearly that God created this earth. We human beings are created in his own image and God instructed us to look after his world.

Activities

1 Ecological footprint

You will need: chalk; questions (find examples here: footprintcalculator.org)

Use chalk to mark out some squares on the ground. Get people to listen to the questions in order, and for each one jump forward a small or a large amount depending on their answer. The further you jump, the bigger your ecological footprint.

Talk about how far you jumped. It's important to see how we can contribute to preserving our earth the way God wanted us to in our day-to-day lives.

2 Insect hotel

You will need: tins; wood wool; paper; corrugated cardboard; hay; twigs; rubber bands; wire; wool for decorating

Build an insect hotel from an empty tin. Think about which animals might find shelter in your hotel and place different materials inside the tin accordingly (e.g. wild bees like pipes such as small paper rolls or corrugated cardboard; green lacewings and ladybugs like wood wool; earwigs like hay; butterflies like thin twigs). Fix a wire to the tin so that you can hang it somewhere outside. If you like, you can decorate the tin with colourful wool by winding the wool around the tin.

Talk about how God came up with a multitude of insects. In order to sustain this huge variety of insects, they all need living space. Within the insect hotel in your garden or on your balcony, a few insects can find a new home.

3 DIY beeswax wrap

You will need: fabric; scissors (or pinking shears); beeswax (in the form of pastilles or grated); baking paper; an iron; an ironing board

Cut leftover fabric with scissors or pinking shears (helps to prevent fraying) into squares or rectangles. Place the fabric piece on baking paper and spread the beeswax on the fabric. Place a second layer of baking paper on top. Now iron the whole thing and you will see how the wax melts. Slowly pull the baking paper off and let the cloth dry before using it.

Talk about how these beeswax wraps are a real alternative to clingfilm and aluminium foil. You can use the wraps to cover yoghurt, fruits and vegetables and even bowls. The wrap adjusts itself perfectly into the correct form through our body temperature. And the best part – we produce less waste!

4 Packaging quiz

You will need: a quiz with various questions about the topic of ecological packaging; quiz sheets; pens

Children and adults can fill in your quiz during the activity time, after which they receive the solutions. There should be a child-winner and an adult-winner.

Talk about what you found out during the quiz.

5 BBQ lighters

You will need: egg cartons; some leftover wax; dryer fluff; a pot for melting the wax; knives

Melt the wax over a fire or on a stove. Place the dryer fluff into the empty egg carton and pour the liquid wax on it. Let it dry and then cut the different compartment of the carton apart. There you go, the lighters are done!

Talk about how normally we would throw the egg cartons, the leftover wax from candles and the dryer fluff away. Today, though, we are creating something new out of them – lighters. A small contribution to less waste and recycling of materials.

6 Exchanging ideas

You will need: footprints made of colourful card (or Post-it notes); pens; a big world map

Write ideas or plans for a more sustainable lifestyle on the footprints. Each idea is precious. Hang the footprints in a heart around the world map. At the end of the session, everybody can take a footprint home as a souvenir.

Talk about the ideas people came up with. Discuss and reflect what you can implement in your daily lives. We want to take God's mandate to preserve the earth seriously.

7 Generating energy

You will need: bicycles; bike roller trainers; dynamo; lamp

Fix one or two bicycles on a roller trainer and connect a lamp via the dynamo. The cyclist should be able to see the lamp. You can generate energy yourself with the bicycles.

Talk about how we can generate 'energy' in our daily lives and inspire others. How can we pass on God's love, just like how our energy is being passed on to the cycle lamp?

8 Storing energy

You will need: solar light chain; a box

Place the solar light chain in the box. During the day, the sun will produce electricity when it shines on the solar panel. Store this electricity in a battery. At night, use the battery to feed the light chain. This is the concept for a modern solar system with battery storage.

Talk about how during the day, the sun generates electricity, which can be stored in a battery to provide light in the night. Where can we bring light into the darkness?

9 Greenhouse effect

You will need: two bottles; thermometers

This longer experiment (30 to 60 minutes) visualises the greenhouse effect within two bottles. Fill one bottle with air, the other with CO_2. Place thermometers in both bottles. The temperature will be higher in the bottle containing the CO_2. This experiment enables the group to easily explain what CO_2 does in our atmosphere and why we should avoid it.

Talk about what God might think when he sees how we handle the earth he created.

10 CD hovercraft

You will need: CDs; pop-top caps (e.g. from a washing-up bottle or a drinking bottle); hot glue gun; balloons; decorations (e.g. washi tape, stickers, pens)

Using the hot glue gun, stick the pop-top cap on top of the hole in the middle of the CD. Slip the opening of the balloon over the pop-top cap and inflate the balloon through the hole (alternatively, you can inflate the balloon before putting it over the cap). Now lift the cap and the CD will start to hover. Watch this video for visual instructions: youtube.com/watch?v=DikofrxCiXs.

Talk about how many toys you have at home which are lying around unused. Whom could you cheer up with them? What could be more sustainable gifts for children in the future?

11 Repair café

You will need: people working in the repair café with sewing machines

The ideal situation would be that there is a local repair café around, whose workers can come over and introduce their work at this activity point. Alternatively, you can ask talented sewers to visit Messy Church with their sewing machine to fix broken pieces of clothing. Inform the families beforehand about the possibility to bring clothing along that needs fixing. You can extend this station for other things (bicycles, electronic devices, etc.).

Talk about how clothing is often produced under inhumane conditions. The repair café shows that broken clothing does not have to be thrown but can be fixed. Could we refrain from buying new clothes? How can I reduce my clothing consumption? Whom could I pass clothes on to that are unused or have become too small?

12 Fruit and vegetable obstacle course

You will need: fruit and vegetables (real or made of wood/felt); buckets; traffic cones (or something similar)

Put the fruits and vegetables in order according to their harvest time and the four seasons. Put up a bucket for each season. Each item has to be brought to the correct bucket through the obstacle course. Check if all items ended up in the correct bucket.

Talk about which fruits and vegetables grow during which season. Which fruits and vegetables do we eat during which season? Show your knowledge! Transporting fruits and vegetables a long way is not good for our earth.

13 Pray for the world

You will need: candles; small glasses as candle stands; a cross; matches; posters and pictures of humans and animals affected by climate change

Show people and animals affected by climate change on posters and pictures. Invite the visitors to pray silently and light a candle.

Talk about how many humans, animals and plants suffer from the consequences of climate change. Here you can light a candle and pray for them. Of course, you can also pray for our world, for those people responsible and for ourselves, so that we take our responsibility towards our world seriously.

Celebration time

Mini-theatre
The host (H) and a garden leek (L), whose roots are his hair and to whom two eyes are fixed, have a chat.

H: Welcome to Messy Church! Great to have you all here. Today our topic is 'Holy in love with God's world!'

L: Hi hi! (H) is in love. (H) is in love. Is it still a secret or may everybody know?

H: Yes, I am in love indeed.

L: With your husband/wife, right?

H: Of course with him/her. Otherwise, we wouldn't be married! But I also love my children.

L: And I love my mummy- and daddy-leek.

H: Yes, and you can also love snow, the forest, nature and yummy food.

L: But not leek soup!

H: And I am in love with something else too.

L: With something else?

H: YES – I am in love with God's world! (*lift the sign with the words 'Holy in love with God's world'*)

L: You're only saying so because it's today's topic!

H: No – I am fascinated by this world that God created and that's why I love it!

L: (H) is in love! (H) is in love! He/she loves God's world.

Floor picture creation

Give different animals (from wood, Lego, Duplo, etc.), plants, flowers, stones and soil to a few adults and children. Spread a white cloth in the middle of your space.

In the very beginning, when there was nothing, absolutely nothing, no world and nothing else – you can't even imagine that. But God was already there.

Place a candle in a glass in the middle.

When God created the universe and the earth, he spoke into the nothingness: Let there be light! And so – just like lightning – it got bright.

Spread a yellow cloth above the candle and a black one below the candle.

What gives us light during the day? – The sun.

Place something to represent sun rays on the cloth.

But God also created some lights to brighten up the darkness in the night. What light shines in the night? – The moon and the stars.

Place something to represent the moon and stars on the dark cloth.

Then God first created things that don't have life: water and land, earth and sand, stones.

Place a blue cloth (water), earth, sand and stones in the middle.

It took a really long time until God was done with all of this, not only creating our planet earth but also the universe. Maybe it even took millions of years. But for God it was only a few days.

And then, God created something absolutely spectacular: God brought life to the earth. He started out with plants: grass, beautiful colourful flowers, bushes, trees.

The volunteers bring flowers and small plants with roots and plant them in the earth.

Then, God created the animals: the very tiny ones – earthworms, centipedes, ants, bugs – and then also the big ones. Plants and animals everywhere across the earth.

The volunteers bring animals (or pictures of animals) and place them in the water or on land.

But God saved the best for last.

Place a mirror wrapped in a brown cloth in the middle. One or more volunteers come forward and uncover it.

In the end, God created humankind, you, me and everyone else. In the Bible we read:

Place the word-card with the text from Genesis 1:27 next to the mirror. A child can read it aloud.

> So God created mankind in his own image; in the image of God he created them; male and female he created them.

God created us in his own image. He loves us so much. He intended us as his counterpart. And it is his wish that we see each other as counterparts as well and treat each other fairly. In addition, he gave us a mandate.

Place the word-card with the text from Genesis 1:28 in the middle. An adult can read it aloud.

> God blessed them and said to them, 'Be fruitful and increase in number; fill the earth and subdue it. Rule over the fish in the sea and the birds in the sky and over every living creature that moves on the ground.'

It is our task to cultivate and to preserve planet Earth. To take care of it and to ensure that nature, plants and animals are doing well. We all enter this world, walk upon it and leave our footsteps on it.

Place a few footsteps symbolically on the floor picture, since not everyone will fit on it!

Maybe we can all be a little more aware and careful about what kind of traces we leave on this planet and on God's creation. We should be 'holy' in love with God's world. We should cultivate it in accordance with his wishes and treat each other fairly.

Prayer

God created planet Earth, with us and everything else, so beautifully. We want to thank him for this. Today, we will do this a little wilder – with a battle call prayer. The leader calls: 'Give me a T!', everyone else calls: 'T'. Then, 'Give me an H!' – 'H'. And so forth with A – N – K – S. In the end, all call out together, 'THANKS, THANKS, THANKS!'

Song suggestion

'He's got the whole world in his hands'

Meal suggestion

Since the topic is sustainability, it's a good opportunity to cook vegetarian food and to discuss our meat consumption. An example could be vegetable or noodle soup, with rice pudding and apple sauce for dessert.

The Netherlands

Nelleke Plomp

Nelleke Plomp is national coordinator of kliederkerk (Messy Church) at the Protestant Church of the Netherlands.

Four sustainable lessons from kliederkerk

Kliederkerk and sustainability is at first sight not the most logical combination. It takes some out-of-the-box thinking to resist the urge for all kinds of disposable material and unhealthy food, and to integrate long-term planning into your team culture. To be honest, for us as the national kliederkerk team, the environment and thinking green isn't always on our mind. Our programmes contain a lot of wasteful ideas. That is why inspiration from local communities is so important to listen to and help to bring us further on our journey.

Janneke Plantinga is a pioneer at YOURS, a fresh expression of church in Drachten, with a green mind and the incredible gift of turning ideas into practice. She writes:

> Starting a sustainable kliederkerk wasn't our goal when we started a fresh expression of church, a few years ago in a disadvantaged neighbourhood in the north of the Netherlands. Yet that is what happened. Read our story and four lessons we learned by doing.

Lesson 1: A rent-free location gives freedom. You are independent from money raisers, which helps secure continuity.

Our first kliederkerk meeting was in December just before Christmas. We rented a space in a ward meeting house. We advertised a lot and there were many promises from families who would come. But only three families came. A disappointment. The turnout also remained low at the next two meetings. We decided to move to the playground opposite the building. Kliederkerk in the open air. This turned out to work well. Many children arrived. People passing by were chatting. Not only did we find a better location, but we are now saving costs for rent.

Lesson 2: Opt for activities that don't cost money. Use items that you have or can borrow yourself. This reduces your footprint and means you use items for longer.

As a volunteer within the church I was used to having money available for craft activities for the children. We wanted to do this differently within the kliederkerk. Why should we all buy stuff when there is so much available for free? We take this into account when preparing the assignments of kliederkerk. We do all our activities with things that we have at home (ball, pawns, skipping rope, buckets) or what we can borrow from our network. This means, among other things, that we organise a maximum of two crafts. Working with freely available material is sustainable, it is convenient because we never know the turnout in advance and it stimulates our creativity.

Lesson 3: Choosing healthy and sustainable food is a step-by-step process. It helps to know your group and let this inform the choices you make.

Eating together is central to kliederkerk. The best thing is if everyone brings something to eat and you share it with everyone. We run into two things in deprived areas. One: many participants are in debt or in debt restructuring and have no financial means to take anything with them. And two: people often have an unhealthy lifestyle. Many families do not consistently eat three meals a day and certainly not a hot meal every day. They often also lack the knowledge and experience to cook healthy food. We therefore opt for a different approach: offering families a free and healthy meal at kliederkerk. We have the food cooked by people from our network and the church in the neighbourhood. We also invite them to eat. This creates contacts between kliederkerk participants and the chefs, who can enthusiastically explain what they have made. In this way the families learn healthy and easy recipes. In practice, this is a path that we take in small steps. We strive for as many fresh products as possible and as little (plastic) waste as possible, but that is still quite a challenge.

Lesson 4: Being a church together costs nothing. Open your house to prepare the kliederkerk together or to eat together.

We organise kliederkerk with only volunteers. There is no paid employee involved. The entire team is responsible and not dependent on one person. The great thing is that we started with a core group of three women, but after a short time our men and children also got a role.

So we organise kliederkerk with families for families. Everyone does the task that suits him or her. One makes flyers, another makes an attribute for the celebration, a number of teenagers enjoy helping to portray the story while another teenager devises and guides fun games. This created a strong connection with families and we started working together more often. For example, we regularly eat together with the families (everyone brings something). Thanks to this institution a sustainable form of church is created. Because believing and living together is also being a church!

New Zealand

Jocelyn Czerwonka

 Jocelyn Czerwonka was Messy Church coordinator for the diocese of Waiapu and is a national team member of Messy Church New Zealand. She previously worked as the youth facilitator for Waiapu and wrote and led the 'Faith Project' based on The Five Marks of Mission (anglicanyouth.org. nz/thefaithproject/thefaithproject).

Currently in the diocese of Waiapu in New Zealand, we are working on adapting our 'Faith Project' (which is based on the Five Marks of Mission) to a context suitable for Messy Church. We are excited about 'Going Wild' with the Fifth Mark of Mission 'Care of Creation'. We've already had fun with 'Care of Creation' Messy Church sessions and others such as celebrating St Francis, Messy Church pet blessings, planting seeds and gardens and more. We love finding ways to explore and appreciate the outdoors and God's creation such as 'pancakes in the park' and 'wild art creations'.

Many of you have already met Ollie the Messy Church Kiwi and some of his friends who have found their way to different parts of New Zealand and around the world, including Kili with Dr Dave and Piki with Lucy Moore. Ollie and friends are very much ambassadors for us, representing the wonderful opportunities to know Jesus through Messy Church, and also the importance of caring for God's creation. In the wild, only 5% of Kiwi chicks survive, and so to protect this endangered species, dedicated Kiwi hatcheries have been established to raise Kiwi chicks to an age and weight that enables them to survive in the wild.

It's our hope that as we explore more about looking after God's creation and 'going wild' at Messy Church that we will all be amazing ambassadors for God and his amazing creation in all we do.

Oh, and if you need more information about Ollie the Messy Church Kiwi – he has his own facebook group: facebook. com/groups/1841858582580810

The Five Marks of Mission	
Telling our story	Proclaim the good news of the kingdom
Growing in faith	Teach, baptise and nurture new believers
Serving others	Respond to human need by loving service
Standing up	Seek to transform unjust structures of society, challenge violence of every kind, and pursue peace and reconciliation
Caring for creation	Strive to safeguard the integrity of creation and sustain and renew the life of the earth.

Julie Guest

Julie Guest is vicar of Te Awamutu Anglican Parish in the North Island of New Zealand. She has been a Messy Church enthusiast for some years and has been involved with setting up three Messy Churches in different areas. She is also a passionate environmentalist and has had an involvement with 'Care of Creation' modules as part of New Zealand's Faith Project for young people.

Greening Messy Church

Stickers, glitter, glue, balloons. Are these what you see when you enter a Messy Church room? Do they crop up on your 'to purchase' list when planning your next session? When we are planning Messy Church activities, we are thinking about what will convey the message of Christ this month, what will engage and attract people, and we turn to these known and attractive tools. To have to think of alternatives can be frustrating, especially when you've had a brainwave and you're excited about your plan. For some busy Messy Church team members, it may even be a challenge too far.

So I want to suggest that the first step in greening a Messy Church is to hold an initial session that establishes the 'why', the reasons for greening your Messy Church. Brainstorm together what the team already knows about environmental damage. Share videos if you have that ability. Feel the shock and pressure of environmental degradation together. Pray, asking God's forgiveness for your part in that damage. Then remind yourselves of the hope we have in God. Our created universe is in God's hands. Your Messy Church can be part of helping people think these issues through for themselves. Pray for guidance as to how and what you can change. Finally, brainstorm a list of alternative resources and places to find them.

This step is essential for your Messy Church, otherwise you will hear comments such as, 'Well I wanted to use balloons for this, but I can't because we're not allowed to,' which sends an unhelpful message that this person is being compelled to comply with someone's else vision. What is more helpful is when you hear someone say, 'I've got a great idea that would have involved balloons. Has anyone got an idea of what I can use instead?'

The next step is to involve those who attend Messy Church in helping to discover new ways to green your Messy Church. Perhaps have a spot during your celebration time where you ask for new ideas, and/or celebrate people's 'green' actions since your last meeting. Has anyone been tree-planting, tidying up a stream edge or changed to solid shampoo to avoid plastic bottles? Celebrate these and thank God for the ideas.

In your tidy-up time, encourage the careful collection of anything that could be reused. I have belonged to a Messy Church that was well resourced financially but people-poor. Tidy-up time was a chore done by an exhausted few. The easiest way was to throw everything out. Sorting things for storage was time consuming. Eventually I suggested that I would take everything home to sort. I didn't have the energy at the time, but it was fine the next day. At your team meeting ask for suggestions to overcome these types of problems.

Experience tells me that one of the strongest places of connection between the secular world and the church in the 2020s is this area of caring for creation. People are surprised to hear that the church has a central tenet of belief that we are to care for creation. Or to put it another way, that we are to love the things God loves in the way that God loves them. As Messy Church was birthed to help connect with those not attending church, I am sure that as we model care for creation in everything we do at Messy Church we will resonate with the younger generation meeting with us. We will open a gate for them to contribute and we all know that contribution leads to belonging.

South Africa

Jean Pienaar

 Jean Pienaar volunteers as a Messy Church coordinator in Johannesburg, South Africa. She enjoys the outdoors and loves to travel. Even if suburban living limits regular encounters with the 'Big 5' (lion, leopard, rhinceros, elephant and buffalo), Jean is invigorated by the electric thunderstorms and the stunning African sunsets. She also learns a lot from her three teenage sons.

South Africa faces many challenges, with the most pressing including corruption, crime, gender-based violence and unemployment. However, it is only by understanding sustainability and the interrelationship of the social and economic environment with the natural environment that any of these issues can begin to be meaningfully addressed. The late Archbishop Desmond Tutu argued that environmental destruction is the human rights challenge of our time, and without immediate action, 'there will be no tomorrow'. In other words, stewardship of the natural environment is crucial to addressing wider societal issues.

Water is a scarce and unequally distributed resource in South Africa. We are also subject to summer heatwaves, devastating fires and flash-floods, which particularly impact people in informal settlements. There are also issues of water pollution (including groundwater pollution), air pollution, limited space for landfill, pressure on natural habitats, desert encroachment and plastics in the oceans – with many of these issues being location-specific. Often, short-term political and economic goals have taken precedence over the natural environment.

The northern suburbs of Johannesburg are privileged to experience the temperate climate of the Highveld, allowing us to enjoy most Messy Church events outside, in our beautiful grounds. Being so close to nature, we are mindful of our natural environment and enjoy having access (along with the resident peacocks) to our green lung in the heart of suburbia. With the pressure for development in Johannesburg, more and more agricultural land on the urban fringe is being used for residential purposes. In fact, 30 years ago, the church grounds where we facilitate Messy Church was farmland. As a result of the pressing suburban development around the church property, the natural habitat of many indigenous creatures such as the giant bull frog and water monitor lizard are threatened. As Messy Church, we engage with the surrounding natural environment in our activities each month, and being in the open air means that nature often forms part of our conversation too. The birdlife in the vicinity enjoys the bird feeders that are a regular favourite Messy Church activity.

The burning of fossil fuels (coal) in the generation of electricity is not only unsustainable (coal is a limited natural resource), but the burning of coal in the power stations contributes to air pollution and increased levels of carbon dioxide in the atmosphere, exacerbating the impact of climate change. The current rolling blackouts when our national energy producer cannot sustain demand means that there are times when whole suburbs are without electricity (and Wi-Fi). Not being reliant on electricity (we make use of the natural lighting and heating) demonstrates to our families our consciousness of the electricity crisis and our commitment to sustainability of energy.

We deliberately recycle wherever possible, limiting waste and embracing responsible stewardship. Many craft activities and games can be adapted to use material that is locally sourced and readily available, thereby reducing the carbon footprint. Food that is not consumed by those present is often given to others on the street who are hungry and homeless. This also demonstrates economic sustainability and contrasts with the corruption that plagues our society.

We also reach out to those in need, reinforcing a culture of giving in an increasingly material world where unemployment has skyrocketed because of the Covid pandemic. The discussion questions linked to our activities do not shy away from the tough questions and challenges facing our country. We believe that it is important that we live an authentic Christianity, creating opportunity to talk about the real, difficult and unresolved issues that we face on a regular basis, and what an appropriate response might be. Based on God's commands to the earliest inhabitants of the garden of Eden to 'work it and take care of it' (Genesis 2:15), we have a responsibility to care for our natural environment – not to abuse it or profiteer from it, and not to destroy it. Awareness creation is critical in this regard.

Ubuntu is a word used in South Africa to describe human relationships. It means that I am because you are. My successes and my failures are bound up in yours. We are made for each other, for interdependence and for relationship. The social and economic challenges are inextricably linked to the natural environment. Furthermore, the challenges our country faces are bigger than us as individuals or families, but together our little efforts can cumulatively make a big difference. Together, we can change the world for the better, one Messy Church at a time.

USA

Johannah Myers

Dr Johannah Myers is the associate director of Messy Church USA and also serves as the director of disciple formation at Aldersgate UMC in Greenville, South Carolina. In 2013, she led Aldersgate in starting a Messy Church and the rest is a very Messy history.

It's a wonderful sight to look around and see tables and chairs, crayons, markers and paper sitting neatly, ready for Messy Church. The activity signs are up. The welcome table is at the ready. It's the calm before the chaos, the precision before the mess. And it's lovely – a sign of hope, a beacon of love. Of course, give it a couple of hours and the room sends off an entirely different signal. Bins filled to overflowing, craft projects left forgotten, plastic table coverings wadded up and tossed away. There's purpose in the mess, sure. But have you ever looked around the room at the end of a Messy Church and wondered, 'Are we making a bigger mess than we should?'

Unfortunately, in many parts of the United States, efforts to recycle or decrease single-use plastics are minimal or even non-existent. It is easy, then, for Messy Churches across the country to fall into the trap of not paying any attention to their environmental impact. How many plastic tablecloths have simply been used once and discarded because they were inexpensive and easy to use? Being a Messy Church that cares about all of creation takes intentionality, especially in communities where creation care is not a focus. Two simple things we talk about in Messy Church USA 'Getting Started' training sessions can make a big difference in a Messy Church's environmental impact.

First, when planning for activities, we encourage Messy Churches to keep things simple. One aspect of this means that before spending money on supplies, we encourage Messy Churches to consider what they already have on hand. We can do so much with simple supplies like paper, crayons, scissors and glue – supplies that can be used multiple ways. Leftover supplies from one activity can become the foundation for another activity at another Messy Church as well. Our first ever Messy Church at Aldersgate United Methodist Church in Greenville, South Carolina, was the story of David and Goliath. We had cut out cardboard 'giant's' feet for one of our activities but overcalculated how many we would need. For four years, we had a stack of giant feet in our storage room waiting for the perfect Messy Church story to reappear. Sure enough, a Messy Church on following Jesus a few years later saw those giant feet turned into a whole new craft! Those cardboard feet cost us nothing as we used recycled cardboard boxes to make them.

Being intentional with what supplies we buy versus what supplies we reuse requires organisation in between each Messy Church. If a team has no clear sense of what supplies they have on hand to use, they are more likely to purchase things they do not really need. Having an organised space may seem completely unrelated to creation care, but knowing what you have means you are more likely to reduce, reuse and recycle!

A second, simple way Messy Churches can be good stewards comes in how they plan for their meal each month. Most of our time planning for our monthly meals is spent in preparing the meal – what to eat, who's cooking, who's serving. However, we also need to spend time planning what to do with any leftover food. Without a plan, too much food is wasted. Is there a community garden nearby (or even at your church) that could use the compost? At Aldersgate, we offer our leftover food to our Messy families for anyone who would like to take some home. With this simple gesture of hospitality, we are able to offer another meal to our lower-income families without singling them out. We also can help out our super-busy families from any economic background by offering another meal they don't have to worry about. We cut down on waste and we extend hospitality beyond our Messy Church gathering!

It's easy to forget about practising good stewardship in places where creation care isn't practised community-wide. But with intentionality and simple habits, we can reduce our waste – both of supplies and food – and learn to be better stewards of the gifts God provides.

9

Case studies

Greening up the Messy activities

Richard Wise

Richard Wise is rector of Bishopstoke in Hampshire, where he loves taking part in Messy Church, a regular Churches Together service for all ages and Open the Book assemblies. He has particular concerns for peace and justice in the world and the environment. He is married with four sons.

Some years ago, some children's leaders and parents in our church were discussing how long they should keep the craft items children had made before binning them. One person said, 'The learning is in the making,' and so often that's true. Once something is made, it might be treasured for a while, but the main purpose was to learn as you did it. Of course, some things might be particularly creative and even beautiful, so you want to keep them. And other things remind us of what we learned and encourage us to put it into practice. I think of the many aids to prayer that have been made by our children over the years.

Messy Church uses loads of 'stuff', and that's the point, really – it couldn't be any other way. We learn, we create, we remember, we pray through it. You might see many of those things as 'icons', drawing us near to God and reflecting God's presence in the world. We can't do without those things. But we should examine how we use those precious resources that God has provided. Where have they come from? What are they made from? Where can they go when they are no longer needed? And can we sometimes use fewer of them and still have a great Messy Church? 'Reduce, reuse, recycle' is a good way of doing an eco-health check on every Messy Church session, and in some cases we can also think of alternative things to use.

Reduce – We need to ask, do we really need a certain item? Could an activity be done a little more simply but still have the same effect? How about being sparing with the use of glitter? I know children love it, but perhaps paint would be enough on many occasions.

Reuse – Is there anything we could use again before it goes in the bin (or recycling)? If you have space, you can save things that might be helpful in the future, e.g. used plastic margarine tubs. Reuse paper and card wherever you can, and if you have to buy it new, make sure you buy a brand with green attributes.

Recycle – When the session has finished, or we have far too many completed crafts at home, how can we dispose of them in the most responsible way? It might be that some could be reused and others recycled, and we need to get into the habit of sorting those things out carefully. Recycling facilities vary from area to area, but there are sometimes places that will take items that can't be put in your household recycling bin. In my area, that includes milk bottle tops and foil. Felt-tip pens are a 'must' for many Messy Church activities – far better than coloured pencils for a lot of things! But when they run out, they tend to be thrown in the bin. There are recycling schemes that include felt tips, though, so why not see if there's one in your area? Take a look at wastenotwantnotliving.co.uk/editorial/recycle-your-felt-tip-pens-with-bics-writing-instruments-programme.

Alternatives

Plastic is probably the biggest challenge for us, but there are often alternatives. You could make a point of getting paper plates, cups and straws, and wooden beads. Sometimes a cardboard tube can be used instead of a cup. I remember an activity which involved making a widow's clothes out of cut-up plastic bin bags – and they looked great! But I wonder if we could have made do with newspaper and had almost as good an effect. No one would have needed to know what the original idea was!

An essential for Messy Churches is sticky tape – children can get through loads of it! But in some cases masking tape could be a good alternative. Glue is another 'must', but you can get eco-friendly varieties, and 100% recyclable glue sticks, and you can also get plastic-free glitter – at a price! And what about balloons? Biodegradable ones aren't as eco-friendly as they might sound, but for some activities other things might do the trick. You can find some ideas at ecofreek.com/biodegradable/biodegradable-balloons.

And then there's the meal. I know it's hard to get the amount of food right, and we don't want anyone going without. But we can still 'reduce': why not think of ways of serving food so that people get the amount they think they can eat? And 'reuse': if there's leftover food it can be given away or taken home by team members and eaten. And 'recycle': make sure there's always a food-waste bin available if you have a collection in your area.

Some of this might seem like a huge adjustment to how we do things, but once we get into the swing of it and build up resources it will get easier. We also have to remember what effect it will have if we all start to make these changes. Here are some websites for eco-friendly craft resources:

- greenecofriend.co.uk/eco-friendly-craft-materials
- peacewiththewild.co.uk

- ecoglitterfun.com
- ecostardust.com

I hope they encourage you to see that this change is possible!

Seasonal Messy Church

Cameron Breward

Cameron Breward, 14, is a young Messy Church leader. He also helps lead the Young Messy Leaders' Zooms.

Our Messy Church is in Chelmsford, Essex, in the south of England. Twenty to thirty people normally come and it is run by Helen Vass. During lockdown we did Messy Church at home, organised five face-to-face meetings and two Messy Church self-directed trails.

The face-to-face sessions were outside. In July we celebrated Easter, as we'd been under heavy restrictions back in April. In September, we had our 'Picnic with God'. In October, we had Harvest with time slots. In December we did 'Exploring Christmas'. One self-directed trail was about God's love for us at Easter and involved heart-bombing, and in May the second trail was on the theme of Pentecost.

We ran the sessions when we able to, working around Covid-19 restrictions. We went outside because we could sing, act our Bible stories and use our natural space. We used an outside grassy area in the churchyard. The best thing about being outside is space and being able to sing, particularly at a time when singing inside wasn't allowed. The biggest challenge outside is trying to be heard. By being outside, you're more part of God's creation.

Christians should care about the planet because it is God's creation and we should care for it. I would say to anyone that the opportunity to meet with God outside should be grasped with both hands.

A Messy family camp

Greg Ross

 Greg Ross is married to Vicki and they have three adult children. He has worked for the church for 35 years as a pastor, youth and families minister and ordained minister of the word. He loves making music, reading and has recently rediscovered the joys of cycling. He is passionate about making sure the church is as open and welcoming for all people in the way that Jesus demonstrated. He loves Messy Church.

In 2018 in Western Australia, St Augustine Uniting Church from Bunbury started a summer holiday Messy extra by offering a 'get close to God in nature' camping experience at the beach in Busselton. We are fortunate that the Uniting Church in Australia has a campsite (tents, caravans and camper vans only, no built accommodation) with direct beach access set in the midst of a wildlife corridor. The site allows us to demonstrate the five core values of Messy Church in a day-to-day lived experience. Everything we do and say tries to offer people an example of what it is to live in a friendship with the risen Christ, extend hospitality to one another, be as creative as we can in every part of our lives, welcome all those of every age who attend, especially extended family members of Messy Church families, and celebrate being in the wonder of creation.

The whole site has an 'eco' theology and philosophy, with only trees and plants that are native to the area growing, a focus on recycling and the use of eco chemicals for cleaning. It also has an environmentally friendly water-treatment system, as the land sits within the nature conservancy area for the endangered western ringtail possum, who live on site along with varieties of native birdlife including the brilliant splendid fairy-wrens and the native skinks who love to sun themselves on the pathways.

As people are not accommodated in buildings, every person and household who comes to stay or visit the site is walking, sleeping, creating and living that much closer to this ancient land upon which the Nyoongar peoples have walked with God for more than 60,000 years.

Messy Church summer camp happens over 18 days (including three weekends) and people come for as much or little of that time as they can manage. We offer sponsorships for households who cannot afford to have a 'holiday' and provide tents and sleeping mattresses for those who do not have their own equipment.

The programme is deliberately low-key so that households of all shapes and sizes have time to reconnect with each other and connect with God. Our team provides sporting equipment, some basic refreshments and craft materials, and we encourage people to go wild. Some people are enthusiastic about sports and play volleyball, basketball, cricket, totem tennis and croquet; they can swim, fish, dive or laze in the tranquil bay waters. Other people are into walking and bike riding and spend time exploring the trails along the bay. Others are content to share food and conversation over jigsaw puzzles or craft activities. There is no daily time schedule for people to attend – it's a holiday!

People are also encouraged to use low-waste food packaging onsite and to recycle as much as possible into the correct bins. Last year over the 18 days we were able to recycle hundreds of drink containers using the 'containers for change' programme running in Western Australia, which was used to help people attend at little or no cost.

Every other day, we provide an option for people to come to together for a creative 'messy' activity based on discovering God in nature and relearning how to care for God's gift of creation. Some evenings people are invited to bring their chairs, tables and rugs and gather on one of the lawn areas to watch a family movie together, which is often the topic of discussion afterwards while sharing a drink. Other evenings nothing much happens and people rediscover the wonder of playing table games or sitting and talking together without technology.

On two or three of the weekends, various Messy Church teams from across the state work together to run an outdoor 'Messy Church' where themes vary from 'Jesus and the ocean' or 'Caring for creation' or 'The outdoor parables' or 'Following Jesus in other cultures', to name a few from the past year or two. Teams are encouraged to use as little plastic or human-made products as possible in our creative work and to make as much as possible of what is done or created from recycled or natural materials. As we continue to build our relationships with the first peoples (*Nyoongar*), we hope to have them leading us at Messy Church summer camp as we discover again what it is to go wild with God in the great South Land of the Holy Spirit.

Living life as an eco-friendly household

Kathy, David and Jonathan Bland

Kathy, David and Jonathan Bland have been Messy Church leaders in rural Herefordshire for ten years. Kathy and David are part of the Messy Church Trainers team and Jonathan is founder of the International Messy Young Leaders group.

To begin with, we'll be honest that we don't have a perfectly eco-friendly lifestyle. We do our best and we actively think about changes we can make and regularly make them. We love an easy win, which for us is about making easy, permanent changes. Once we've made them, we don't have to keep thinking about them – we win!

We like long-term changes – here are some of ours. Some of them are tiny and some are enormous, but they are all possible for us. It's really important not to judge other people about the choices that are possible for them; we're all different. Hopefully our changes might spark some ideas for you.

Jonathan doesn't use shampoo (gasp!) and never has done. He might, at any point, decide that he will, but he's 14 and he never started. If you try to give up using shampoo, it can be really hard – your hair panics at the lack of chemicals and it can take about six weeks to balance out. If you never start using shampoo, your hair uses its natural oils to keep itself naturally beautiful and healthy. Water is great for washing hair. Kathy does use shampoo but in the form of shampoo bars – no plastic bottles.

We have our milk delivered in glass bottles from the dairy. It's not plastic. It's easy. It costs more but we've decided we can do it. We also use loose tea to cut down on plastic in teabags and loose coffee in a cafetiere – no coffee pods for us. We always take a reusable cup when we go out so we can refill it.

Where we can, we cook from scratch to cut down on single-use plastic packaging. We make our own bread, grow some of our own vegetables and use a veg box scheme to access locally grown and unpackaged vegetables. We try to choose tins, glass and loose items over single-use plastic. A couple of years ago we gave up single-use plastic for Lent and during that time we learned how extraordinarily difficult it is to do this. If we cook everything from scratch and buy from greengrocers and other local shops, it is just about possible but often there is hidden plastic in the supply chain – our local shops are removing packaging that we don't see, so we can only do our best. We definitely can't manage it all the time, but we recycle and re-use as much as we can.

We changed both our cars to electric ones. They are more expensive so we bought second-hand. To start with, we bought one electric car but we loved it so much that when our diesel car wore out we bought another electric one. We are now electric car evangelists, so if you need convincing, get in touch!

We re-use things. Messy Church is great for doing this. We save up recycling for junk modelling and are often thinking, 'What can we do with that?' We often enlist the help of our Messy Church families to save up tubes and bottles for a creative activity. We also went on a Messy Church outing to our local recycling centre to check we were all recycling the right things – it was fun and we learned loads.

We are food-waste warriors. At home, we try not to throw food away, which means eating leftovers, preserving things and only buying what we need. On a community scale, we pick up supermarket surplus food and 'food share' it, which means we give away food in partnership with the food bank to anyone who wants it. This has saved tonnes of food in the last year, as well as saving people money on their food bills. In our small town, our bakery and all three supermarkets are joining in with us. Sometimes this has meant learning how to use a glut of things all at once – eggs, pears, avocados, bags of salads. We're getting creative at responding to the challenge. When we do have to throw food away, we have two eco-routes for it. Our chickens love to eat leftovers and our compost bin loves peelings.

When Jonathan was a baby, we didn't buy baby equipment (apart from a car seat). We created a supply chain of baby clothes which were passed to us and we then passed on to friends with slightly smaller children. We used second-hand (almost) everything so that we weren't filling the world with more stuff. We used washable nappies and were fortunate to be able to breastfeed. Having children is a huge factor in environmental impact, but we did it as lightly as we could. Kathy (the only woman in the house) uses a menstrual cup for her periods. She is super proud of all the sanitary products that haven't gone to landfill (or the sea) on her account.

We holiday in the most eco-friendly way we can, which usually means camping in our tents. We have been interrailing and we really loved it. We don't go on cruises and we avoid flying. We often go on holiday really close to where we live to save road miles.

We try to use things for as long as we can instead of buying new. We ask, 'Do we need this?' a lot and then often don't buy it. We try to 'buy' experiences rather that stuff – doing things over having things.

Our top tips:

1 Mostly just don't buy stuff. Use what you have and keep using it or give it to someone who will use it.
2 Be imaginative about using other people's stuff. Enjoy second-hand and charity items, sharing food, cooking up a glut and creative junk art.
3 If you can do a big thing, then do it: solar panels, electric car, air source heat pump, eco fuel tariff. We are trying to steward our resources in the best way we can.
4 Make small and lasting changes to your habits – take your own cup, buy loose over packaged.
5 If you are having a baby, consider not using shampoo on them – ever!
6 Book a trip to your recycling centre to become more effective recyclers. Even better if you can make it a Messy Church outing!

Messy pilgrimage

Bob Jackson

 Bob Jackson was a government economic adviser in the 1970s. After 20 years as a vicar, he spent another 20 helping churches to grow. Pottering about in retirement, he's devised two pilgrimage routes ending up in the Derbyshire village of Eyam, where he lives. He loves meeting pilgrims who have had a wonderful time on their long walks.

Jesus and his family went on a pilgrimage every year – to Jerusalem for the Feast of the Passover. While returning from that pilgrimage when Jesus was twelve, his parents left for home without their eldest son, finding him eventually in the temple courts. Christians have always gone on pilgrimages to holy places, partly to holiday and partly to experience God in a new way. There has been a big revival in pilgrimage in recent years, including many non-religious people looking for a spiritual experience. You may be quite surprised that people who would never go to a church service would be happy to join in with a Christian pilgrimage – or to go on one by themselves – perhaps to find themselves again after a spell of stress or pressure.

Going on pilgrimage is a great way for families to bond, explore faith and meet with God together. Mary, Joseph and their children went on pilgrimage with a large group of friends and extended family. A whole Messy Church family going on pilgrimage together can be a particularly rich experience. Though, if you do this, please remember to count all the children before you leave your equivalent of Jerusalem!

When life got too thronged and exhausting for Jesus, he escaped up a mountain to pray and recharge his batteries. Many of us find this works for us too. Millions of people have discovered during the Covid lockdowns that walking in the great outdoors is spiritual therapy, raising their sense of well-being and ability to cope with life.

A pilgrimage is spiritual fun – holidaying with God to a holy place which is, for the pilgrim, a thin spot between heaven and earth. The journey there takes us out of our routines, making us more receptive to God the creator, more aware of God the Saviour who journeys through life with us. The destination is a special place for encountering God and taking stock of life. Returning home, pilgrims will hopefully have been changed and strengthened to live life better, with a new experience of walking through God's world to empower and inspire them through what is to come.

Children, especially those with limited experience of being immersed in the countryside, will understand, love and care for the planet better through experiencing nature's moods, beauty and complexity. And many will respond to the God who made the natural world. Through walking further than they had imagined possible, children will also gain a sense of accomplishment and a new confidence in their own ability to navigate God's world.

In practical terms, there are normally three intertwining elements in the pilgrimage journey. First is the stripping out of everything except the simple act of walking itself. This clears the mind to regroup, recover self-awareness and be reconnected to our surroundings. Second is the journey through the scenery, flora and fauna of creation, which enables us to meet the creator just as we meet a great painter through studying their art. And third is entering churches along the way, finding peace in buildings specifically designed to be meeting places between God and humans. Many churches are living expressions of centuries of faith, connecting us to our deep roots and Christian heritage.

A pilgrimage does not need to be ascetic – it can be full of discovery, joy, fun, picnics, tea shops, ice creams, laughter, all celebrating the goodness of God, the joys of his world and the privilege of being allowed out in it.

You do not need to walk 500 miles along the Camino de Santiago de Compostela to go on a pilgrimage. There are many wonderful and much shorter pilgrimage routes in the UK and elsewhere. Check them out at britishpilgrimage.org/routes. Many are time-honoured routes connecting to our great cathedrals or our ancient saints. Some take several days, while some can be walked in one day. But some routes are quite new. For example, I've designed two new pilgrimage routes designed to be enjoyed by families as well as adults and young people. They centre on the Peak District 'plague' village of Eyam, where I live. They can be walked in three to four days or else in a series of day trips with the help of our guidebooks. Check out peakpilgrimage.org.uk.

PART III

SESSION OUTLINES

10

Where were you when?
(in-person session)

Martyn Payne

 Formerly part of BRF's Messy Church team, Martyn Payne is a gifted storyteller whose previous books, *The Big Story* (2011) and *Creative Ways to Tell a Bible Story* (second edition, 2022), demonstrate the variety of approaches he uses to bring the Bible alive for children and adults alike. He is passionate about the blessing that comes when generations explore faith together.

Job 38—41

Bible story

And now, finally, God answered Job from the eye of a violent storm. [God] said: 'Why do you confuse the issue? Why do you talk without knowing what you're talking about? Pull yourself together, Job! Up on your feet! Stand tall! I have some questions for you, and I want some straight answers.

'Where were you when I created the earth?... Who decided on its size?... Who came up with the blueprints and measurements? How was its foundation poured and who set the cornerstone, while the morning stars sang in chorus and all the angels shouted praise? And who took charge of the ocean when it gushed forth like a baby from the womb?…

'Have you ever ordered Morning "Get up!"; told Dawn "Get to work!"… Have you ever got to the true bottom of things, explored the labyrinthine caves of deep ocean? Do you know the first thing about death? Do you have one clue regarding death's dark mysteries?…

'Do you know where Light comes from and where Darkness lives so you can take them by the hand and lead them home when they get lost? Why, *of course* you know that! You've known them all your life, grown up in the same neighbourhood with them!

JOB 38:1–21 (MSG, abridged)

Pointers

The story of Job is a very ancient tale from around the fourth or fifth century BC. It's all about how human beings struggle with questions to do with undeserved suffering. Job himself suffers terribly and is full of questions as he tries to make sense of what has happened to him – the loss of his home, his health and his family. His wealth and his status did not save him; his good life and faith in God did not stop the terrible things that happened to him. The story is from long ago but it is nevertheless a story for our time too, as we struggle with our unfair world, with global pandemics and natural disasters.

Friends try and reason with Job, but their words don't help. Their words are well-meaning but fail to connect with what Job is experiencing. And then in chapter 38 God begins to speak. God answers Job's questions with questions of God's own. In fact, question after question comes for almost four whole chapters! And God's questions serve to remind Job and us of who we are and who God is.

The questions focus on the wonders of creation which are not of our making and in fact are far beyond anything we could ever imagine, control or understand. What we have in these chapters is a poetic retelling Genesis 1 – unpacking the variety, splendour and majesty of creation. Job is being asked to look again at the big picture of this world in all its beauty, and in this way put his own life into perspective. The world does not revolve around him and what happens to him, and that is true for us too. This planet isn't all about us. God did choose to create us in his likeness and that is amazing, but that should not lead us to get things out of proportion. We are created to be caretakers of this amazing universe and not behave as if it were all there to serve our needs.

We are not more important than the earth. Its future and ours are intimately connected, which is why the climate emergency is a spiritual crisis not just an unfortunate byproduct of human development. God's questions to Job begin to put this right by reminding him of the mystery and marvel of how this world works. So many things are beyond our knowing: we can't control the weather, the tides, the winds, the Earth's light sources, its storms or its seasons. The ways of wildlife too are a wonder and God's questions finally focus down in chapters 40 and 41, like a powerful episode of *Planet Earth*, on the wonderful descriptions of 'Behemoth and Leviathan' – the hippopotamus and a sea monster respectively – two of the many wonders of the natural world.

We are not God. We don't know everything and even what we do know is a gift from God anyway. Creation is marvellous without us and so we should honour it and look after it with great humility.

#discipleship: team

Messy health check
How will this Messy Church session increase everyone's appreciation of our home planet and the marvellous variety of flora and fauna upon it? How will wonder, thankfulness and responsibility be woven into all that we share?

Messy team theme
- Invite everyone to name the most amazing natural phenomenon that they have experienced and share how it made them feel
- Talk about how the activities for this Messy Church can contribute to better caring for God's world
- Does anyone have a story of how facing suffering brought them closer to God in the end, as it did for Job?

How does this session help people grow in Christ?
Job's 'comforters', as they are often called, failed to help Job and answer his many questions. Maybe this was because they insisted that they knew 'the right answers' and were trying to fix Job rather than understand him. There are no neat answers to the mystery of suffering, to natural disasters and to illness, pain and grief. Suffering can't be explained; it needs to be entered into – and that's exactly what Christians believe God did in the life, death and coming to life again of Jesus. In our Bible reading, God asks Job if he knows the first thing about death and its mysteries, and indeed where light and darkness live. In Jesus, God who created light, experienced darkness and death: Christ was at the very beginning when the stars sang with the angels to celebrate creation. All things were created through Christ and so like Job we can encounter God in all aspects of creation... and that includes Behemoth and Leviathan too!

Mealtime card
- What is your favourite wild animal and why?
- What do you like best about the environment where you live?
- What evidence have you seen of how our world is suffering at the moment?
- What are your top three things that would make this planet a better place to live on?

Take-home idea
In today's Bible story God asks lots of questions – and God wants us to ask questions too! God has given us enquiring minds; it's one of the ways we are like God.

At home, challenge everyone to come up with four or five questions about the world. Get these written down on paper and put them into a bowl which you could place perhaps onto a map of the world. Every main mealtime this coming week, each member of the family should pull out a question in turn to ask everyone else. And each question might hopefully lead on to further conversations about green issues (and indeed some questions might need internet help!) For example:

- How many different sorts of cloud formations are there?
- How deep is the deepest ocean/the highest mountain?
- Where is the driest desert in the world?
- How many sorts of butterflies can you name?
- Which is the fastest creature on Earth?

After each question time, pause for a prayer of thanksgiving to God for giving us such an amazing world.

Question to start and to end the session
Is there anything that leaves you speechless with wonder whenever you see it?

#discipleship:extra

'Creation is not all about me, it is about God!' Maybe this is the one big lesson that Job learned when he listened to God's litany of rhetorical questions.

Why not explore the information and stories on the websites of Christian Climate Action (christianclimateaction.org), Tearfund (tearfund.org/stories/2020/09/why-christians-should-care-about-climate-change) or A Rocha (arocha.org.uk) and find out more about how people are campaigning to look after our planet better. Find out about local and national campaigns; and you might even be able to invite someone to come and speak at a Messy discipleship extra organised on this theme.

Social action

Following the pandemics of recent years, there has been much talk of 'building back better' and finding 'a new normal'. This includes fresh thinking about how we care for our environment and how we tackle the climate emergency. Talk about some possible responses to this over the meal at your Messy Church session and decide on some action for the future, such as doing one of the following:

- planting a Messy Church wildflower garden that attracts pollinators
- organising a regular local litter pick in the area
- twinning your Messy Church toilet or bin with another around the world
- collecting particular items for recycling and raising money for charity, e.g. ink cartridges, plastic bottle tops, etc.
- exploring what is involved in creating and using eco-bricks; then work on making a Messy Church seat or table for future gatherings.

Activities

1 Cloud making

You will need: water; a glass jar with a lid; hairspray; blue food colouring; three or four cubes of ice

'Who has wisdom to count the clouds? Who can tip over the water jars of the heavens?' (Job 38:37). Heat up water (which you've already coloured blue) and pour the warm water into a glass jar about halfway up. Quickly spray hairspray into the jar and immediately put on the lid. Place three or four pieces of ice on top of the lid of the jar. Watch a cloud form in the jar. After a while, release the cloud.

Talk about the importance of clouds for our weather systems and the different types of clouds there are. God has given us a planet that has just the right balance of water and sunshine, cold and heat, to sustain life. We unbalanced this at our peril.

2 Starting a composting toilet

You will need: three five-gallon buckets; a piece of plywood; a wood saw; screws and screwdriver; organic material from a nearby wooded area; branches; a tarpaulin

'Who cuts the channel for the torrents of rain… to satisfy a desolate wasteland and make it sprout with grass?' (Job 38:25, 27). This activity requires DIY cooperation between adults and children. It might be helpful to prepare some elements in advance. This activity is only the first step toward making a composting toilet but should provide plenty to do and lots to talk about. Perhaps this could be a special activity for a group of older children and some adults. Or for groups with younger children, you might just focus on the collecting of the natural composting dust and the modesty shelter.

On your plywood, mark a circle which should be the circumference of the top of a bucket. An adult (with a precise and steady hand!) should cut out this hole in the wood. This will become the toilet seat.

Next, using a wood saw, cut the top 4 to 6 inches off one of the buckets. This will serve as a flange to which the seat is attached, allowing it to slip inside a second bucket. The bottom part of the cut bucket can be recycled, for example as a planter. This could become another creative activity focus for the group, providing a place for sweet-smelling flowers beside your composting toilet.

The third bucket needs to be filled with sawdust, chipped wood, chopped straw, cereal hulls, crumbled bark and dead leaves to be an absorbent carbon-rich organic mix. This needs to be collected from an outdoor area. The contents of the composting toilet needs covering with several cups or handfuls of this matter after each use. This will also effectively prevent odours.

When the receptacle bucket is full, transfer the flanged toilet seat to the now empty sawdust bucket which then becomes the receptacle.

The toilet contents need to be buried in a 'composting chamber'. For this, another group will need to dig a hole away from where people are and any water sources. Once the toilet contents are in the chamber, cover it with a fresh layer of sawdust to prevent odours and present an aesthetic appearance. Clean and sanitise the empty receptacle and dry in sunlight. This bucket, after filling with clean material, then becomes the sawdust bucket, and the cycle starts over. Composted humanure takes about a year to break down into compost that can be used in your garden.

Although not necessary, urine could be collected separately in a sealable container (such as an inexpensive but sturdy plastic bottle). Because of its high value as a nitrogen source, it can be diluted by 5 parts water and put directly on plants.

Finally, another group could work on building a 'modesty shelter' from branches propped up against a tree and covered with either dense foliage or tarpaulin, to be the site where the composting toilet will be situated for use.

Talk about how good for the environment these toilets are, particularly because they don't use any water. God's creation has 'recycling' built in and this is one way to work with nature in harmony with God.

3 Eco-print dying

You will need: ready-to-dye plain fabric; a basketful of natural plants, foliage and bark; string; mallets or hammers; a source of steam

'Have you commanded the morning... that it might take hold of the skirts of the earth... It is... dyed like a garment' (Job 38:12–14, abridged, NRSV). Lay down your collection of plants, leaves and barks on to half of your fabric, cleaning away any dust or dirt. Fold the other half over it. Pound the fabric. Roll it up tight and wrap it around with string. Place in a bowl above steaming water for as long as possible. Allow it to dry by hanging it up.

Talk about the varieties of colours that God has put into the world for us to enjoy. What are your favourite colours and why?

4 Making static electricity

You will need: a plastic comb; pieces of dry cereal; a half-metre length of thread; sticky tape

'Can you send forth lightnings?' (Job 38:35). Wash the comb to remove oils and dry it thoroughly. Charge the comb by running it through long, dry hair or by rubbing it vigorously on a woollen sweater. Bring it near to a piece of cereal that you have attached to a thread hung from a table or chair. Watch as the electrons in the comb with a negative charge initially attract the neutral cereal but then repel that cereal once it becomes charged.

Talk about invisible powers that we cannot see such as magnetism, gravity and the movement of air as wind. Compare this with the invisible but real power and presence of God in our world.

5 Star to star drawings

You will need: black sugar paper; sticky stars; chalk (this could be a large mural activity)

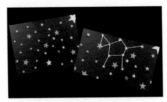

'Can you bind the chains of Pleiades or loose the chords of Orion?' (Job 38:31). Invite people to place stars of different shapes and sizes randomly across the paper's surface. Then ask them to use their imagination to join up those stars to create people, objects and animals in 'the sky at night'. Astrologers down the ages have seen shapes in the stars. What new constellations can your Messy Church family create?

Talk about the billions and billions of stars in God's universe – more than enough for each of us to each have a constellation of our own; marvel at the vastness of God's world.

6 Fir cone feeders

You will need: dried-out pine or fir cones; bird seed; raisins; peanuts; grated cheese; suet or lard; mixing bowl; string; scissors

'Who provides food for the raven when its young cry out to God and wander about for the lack of food?' (Job 38:41). Make-up your bird mix in a mixing bowl. Mix it with your fingers so the fat holds the squishy mess together. Tie some fir cones together with string and then pack them with the sticky mixture. Allow it to set for a short while – in a cool place if possible – and then hang them from a tree.

Talk about how, sadly, there are fewer insects around today for birds to feed on because of climate change, so they need a helping hand. How many different sorts of birds can people name? The gifts of bird-song and birds' colourful plumage are part of the glory of God's world.

7 Basking Behemoths

You will need: paper plates; egg boxes; colouring pens; marshmallow pieces; icing; scissors; glue; bowl of water

'Look at Behemoth, which I made along with you… What strength it has in its loins, what power in the muscles of its belly!' (Job 14:15–16, abridged). The behemoth described in Job 40 is most likely the hippopotamus.

Fold your paper plate in half so it becomes a big mouth that can open. Using icing, attach the marshmallow pieces as teeth on the lower jaw of the mouth. Take two cardboard egg cups from an egg box, cut these in half and attach these to the top of the upper half-plate, to represent two eyes and two ears. Add your own colourful designs to the creature's head. Place this on some water and, as the plate soaks up the water, it should begin to yawn open like a hippopotamus' mouth.

Talk about the hippopotamus, also known as the 'river horse', which is another of God's creatures that sadly is an endangered species because of the loss of its habitat. Talk about the pros and cons of rescuing these creatures by breeding them in zoos or finding ways to preserve them in the wild.

8 No Planet B

You will need: information about the dangers facing our planet from climate change and species loss (for example go to the websites of Christian Climate Emergency, The World Wildlife Fund, A Rocha, or Tearfund – see #discipleship: extra); a large blow-up world; sticky notes; pens

'Then Job answered the Lord, "I am unworthy – how can I reply to you? I put my hand over my mouth"' (Job 40:3–4). This is a prayer station, giving families opportunities to focus on aspects of the climate emergency and the need to care for our planet by turning that into prayers which they stick on the globe.

Talk about what concerns people most about the future of our planet and what actions we can take, including prayer. Christians believe we are called to be stewards of this planet in partnership with God.

9 Creating a sea monster

You will need: a play tunnel; bubble wrap; a variety of cardboard pieces; colourful tissue paper; polystyrene packing of various shapes, sizes and colours; pegs; staplers; a glue gun

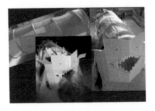

'Can you draw out leviathan with a fish-hook, or press down his tongue with a cord?' (Job 41:1, NRSV). Leviathan is variously understood as a huge sea creature like a blue whale or possibly a massive prehistoric crocodile! God introduces Job to this creature in his conversation with him, presenting it as an example of the wonderful, wild otherness of God's creation.

This is a group activity for the whole Messy Church congregation to work on as they let their imagination run wild as to what Leviathan looked like, by adding to a play tunnel which is its body. Using a variety of junk modelling material as suggested above, build up the monster's appearance with material to represent fins or wings, eyes, mouth, teeth and other appendages! The bubble wrap could be its skin, for example. One inspiration for this could be a traditional dragon as seen at Chinese New Year festivals.

Talk about the huge variety of creatures on earth and the wonders of creation such as those highlighted by TV programmes such as *Planet Earth*. Share stories of what amazes you most about this world's wildlife.

10 Fondant animals

You will need: a quantity of fondant icing; food colouring; dried fruit pieces such as sultanas or raisins; wet wipes to clean hands; paper plates

 'Who has let the wild ass go free... to whom I have given the steppe for its home, the salt land to his dwelling-place?' (Job 39:5–6, NRSV). Throughout chapter 39 we read about wild goats, ostriches, horses and birds of prey. They are all God's gifts to enjoy and care for as part of God's amazing world. In chapter 41:11 God tells Job, 'Everything under heaven belongs to me [God].'

Using the food colouring, create plenty of fondant lumps in different colours, which can then be shaped into animals of all shapes and sizes to be decorated with dried fruit. There are plenty of pictures online of edible animals to inspire, but do allow families to create their own animals, maybe including those which sadly have now become extinct because of our poor care for God's world.

Talk about the delight God has in all that God has made and how we, who are created in God's image, should also share in the joy of creation and not the destruction of this planet.

Celebration

You will need: a 1,000-piece jigsaw; a huge encyclopaedia; an object with lots of sides such as a hexagonal prism (e.g. a many-sided dice); a bowl of water; a pipette or water-dropper

Celebrate your gathering together as church with welcoming conversation about the various activities everyone has been engaged with. What have people enjoyed? What worked well? What caught their interest?

And did anything not work? Or did some go badly wrong?

Things do go wrong in life, we all know that, and the main character in today's story had had a really bad time. He had been pushed to the limits by sadness, sickness and suffering.

I wonder how you react to bad times? We've certainly all had our fair share of these during the recent pandemic years. And some people of course suffered a lot.

As you ask the following questions, invite people to act out or pull faces to match the moods.

Do you sulk maybe? (*pull a sulking face*)

Do you shout out in anger? (*put on an angry face*)

Do you try and blame someone or something for what's happened? (*point the finger*)

Do you lash out at others, often those closest to you? (*shake fists*)

Or do you just go very quiet and keep it all bottled up on the inside? (*fold arms and look down morosely*)

Or is there something else you do?

Job – whose name is spelt like 'job' but pronounced differently – did all these things and something else! He talked to God.

He didn't just talk – he shouted at God, complained to God and got angry with God. The Bible has many examples of angry prayers to God. Don't worry! God can take it. In fact God wants us to express how we really feel. God is always there to listen.

And God certainly had a lot of listening to do as far as Job was concerned, because Job talked, and talked, and talked! He asked lots of questions. He did have friends who tried to help him but mostly they just couldn't get through to him. Maybe Job, in his pain, had forgotten how to listen. That can happen.

But God knows how to listen. God waits patiently while we let all our feelings out.

And then… and then, God spoke. Yes, God speaks to Job and it is with an unexpected answer to all Job's complaints.

God reminds Job of how little Job actually knows!

Invite everyone to take a jigsaw piece from the 1000-piece jigsaw set. Keep hold of the box yourself so you can rattle the remaining pieces to make the following point:

Job has only one piece of the big jigsaw of God's creation. Whereas God holds the whole jigsaw and knows what's really going on.

Show everyone a multi-faceted geometrical figure such as the hexagonal prism or a many-sided dice.

Job only sees one side of the many-sided picture of God's creation, whereas God sees the whole thing and knows it from every angle.

Show everyone a huge encyclopaedia.

Job only has a few scraps of information from the huge encyclopaedia of life in this universe, whereas God wrote the whole book.

Show everyone a bowl of water and then with the pipette or water dropper, drop one drop into it.

Job is aware of only one small drop in the water of the ocean of God's creation, whereas God was there at the beginning, stayed there throughout all the millennia that have already gone by and will be right there on into eternity.

In other words, God reminds Job that it's not all about Job – it's about this whole world and God is ultimately in control of what happens.

Job is stunned into silence. For the first time he starts to really listen. Then God takes him on a magnificent tour of the wonder of life on earth.

As each of the following is mentioned, invite actions and sounds to go with the words:

> **The glory of the clouds in the sky,**
> **The wonder of the stars at night,**
> **The magnificence of the oceans on earth,**
> **The beauty of the sunrise and sunset,**
> **The mystery of birth and death,**
> **The marvel of light and colour,**
> **The majesty of snow and ice,**

The power of lightning and thunder,
The gift of rain.

In other words, God reminds Job about the importance of our climate systems, which sadly many of us have forgotten about and which we have damaged.

And then he moves on to the amazing world of creatures on earth:

The songs of the birds,
The sounds of wild animals,
The life cycle of plants,
The uniqueness of creatures such as the ostriches, birds of prey, oxen and horses.

In other words, God reminds Job that biodiversity and the inter-dependence of life on earth is God's idea – and that too is something we have forgotten about in our day. This world is not all about us.

Finally, God focuses on two magnificent creatures in particular.

Everyone could have a go at finding a way to imitate or become these creatures!

The hippopotamus, which the Bible calls Behemoth, and Leviathan, which is some sort of sea monster – maybe a great whale or a massive prehistoric crocodile.

I wonder what creatures you would say are the most exotic you've ever heard about or possibly seen?

Climate wonder and creation glory are all beyond Job's knowing, beyond Job's power to control and certainly beyond Job's making. No wonder Job ends by telling himself to shut up and listen to God. Only then can everything get back into its proper perspective and Job can begin to understand what has happened to him.

We too need to take a long hard look our amazing world. It's God's world and we are called to care for it, not to mess it up. We are called to love it just like God does. When we do this we will be working with God to create God's kingdom on earth.

Planet care is our primary job on earth and this is the best way we can serve, love and praise God.

Prayer

After listening to God, Job prays a very humble prayer which is the pattern for our prayer today (Job 42:1–6).

Ask people to create a huge circle with two hands, inviting everyone to repeat the following words as their prayer:

Lord God, you can do anything; the whole world belongs to you.

Ask people to bow their heads and hold their hands out to either side, inviting everyone to repeat the following words as their prayer:

Lord God, you know everything; there is so much we don't understand.

Ask people to raise their hands high and to lift up their heads, inviting everyone to repeat the following words as their prayer:

Lord God, you made everything; you are more wonderful than we can imagine.

Ask everyone to look around at everyone and everything in the room, inviting everyone to repeat the following words as their prayer:

Lord God, all of nature is your idea; we're sorry we've not looked after what you have made.

Ask everyone to hold hands with each other (or touch elbows, if the former is not possible), inviting everyone to repeat the following words as their prayer:

Lord God, thank you for asking us to look after your world; we commit ourselves to care for this planet with your help. Amen

Song suggestions
'Bad times won't last' – Fischy Music
'This is how I am feeling' – Fischy Music
'Big big questions' – Fischy Music
'Who's the king of the jungle?' – Annie Spiers
'Who put the colours in the rainbow?' – Paul Booth
'Who took fish and bread?' – Betty Lou Mills
'We plough the fields with tractors' – based on the traditional harvest hymn from the Arthur Rank Centre (arthurrankcentre.org.uk/resources/we-plough-the-fields-with-tractors)

Songs about the environment from Out of the Ark music: outoftheark.co.uk/blog/top-5-songs-about-the-environment

Creation songs using nursery rhyme tunes: ministry-to-children.com/creation-songs

Meal suggestion
Make a big effort to choose home-grown produce and healthy ingredients for whatever meal you choose for this session. In particular, try and avoid anything that has had to travel many air miles before it was sold in this country. You may know of some local allotment holders and so be able to source fresh ingredients from them for a vegetarian meal.

11

Jesus in the wilderness
(online session)

Jonathan Bland, Cameron Breward, Dylan Heydon-Matterface, Sophia Byrne, Della Gassert, Bianca Khoo, Jonte and Adele Voutier (young leaders' team)

During lockdown in 2020, Jonathan Bland from Herefordshire, a teenage Messy Church leader, whose parents both lead Messy Churches in different parts of that very rural county, was in the back seat of the car, having a rant about feeling like the only young Messy leader in existence. His parents suggested contacting the Messy Church team at BRF to see what might be done. Was this in the spirit of passing the buck or divine inspiration? We shall never know. They did get in touch and Jonathan's idea for creating an online group for young Messy leaders was mooted. At the time, most of the BRF Messy Church team was on furlough and things were very stretched, to say the least, but it was such a gift of an idea, especially as it had come, not from an adult deciding what was best for young people, but from the young person himself, that we decided we couldn't not go with it.

We plunged into the safeguarding requirements in order to make sure the online space was as safe as it could reasonably be. And very cheerfully accepted Jonathan's kind offer (ahem, insistence) that he would make the sessions happen himself and not be on the receiving end of adults dishing it out. The deal was, and still is, that BRF sorts out the structural side – the safeguarding, setting up the Zoom, advertising and booking – while the young leaders decide what they're doing and lead it on the day.

Leaders in the plural, as Jonathan was fairly soon joined by another 13-year-old (who has since had to pull out because of other commitments) and two others: Cameron Breward and Dylan Heydon-Matterface, both sons of Messy Church leaders and young leaders in their own right locally. The three of them now coplan and colead the sessions, with adults literally muted. They've been so committed that they also took on responsibilities on the planning and delivery team for the 2022 International Conference.

The regular participants include a dedicated group of young leaders from Melbourne, Australia (hence the odd time of 9.00am UK time – it means the Australians can just about join in, late at night.) These young leaders from Victoria have also led a session on their 'Messy Miners' approach – using Minecraft to explore Bible stories together online.

In February 2021, the cross-continental team devised and led a session on Jesus in the wilderness for the start of Lent, with an emphasis on caring for God's earth. The UK team led the activities and story and the Australians led the 'spicy prayer'. It certainly worked online for an hour's session across continents; it would also work onsite, though the team devised a limited number of activities compared with a normal Messy Church session. Onsite would also be kinder to computer keyboards: it was speedily discovered that flour and electronics don't mix…

Jesus in the wilderness

A Messy Church online session to explore the story of Jesus' temptations and to think about the sort of temptations human beings face in the context of how we treat the world around us.

Part 1

Welcome everyone and set out the theme for today, as above. Tell the first part of the story from Matthew 4:

> Then Jesus was led by the Spirit into the wilderness to be tempted by the devil. After fasting for forty days and forty nights, he was hungry. The tempter came to him and said, 'If you are the Son of God, tell these stones to become bread.'
>
> Jesus answered, 'It is written: "Man shall not live on bread alone, but on every word that comes from the mouth of God."'
>
> MATTHEW 4:1–4

We're going to make bread to remind us of this part of the story. You may need to mix everything together from scratch or you may have brought the dough ready made with you – you can knead it some more while we talk.

You could find a recipe online or use this one:

1 sachet of dry yeast
500 g bread flour
2 tsp salt
2 tsp sugar
300 ml warm water
2 tbsp olive oil

Stir together all the dry ingredients. Add the water and the olive oil. Stir well, then knead. Divide into twelve small blobs. Place on a greased baking sheet and leave to rise for the next part of the session in a warm place. Bake for 10–15 minutes at 240C/220C fan/gas 9.

Talk about

- How are we tempted to make bad choices when it comes to where we get our food from? Do we think about where our food has come from?
- What do you think is unfair about food in the world?
- What do you know about Fairtrade?
- What other organisations do you know about that help food be shared out more fairly?
- What's the most important thing for you about how Jesus thought about food?

Part 2

Tell the next part of the story:

> Then the devil took [Jesus] to the holy city and set him on the highest point of the temple. 'If you are the Son of God,' he said, 'throw yourself down. For it is written: "He will command his angels concerning you, and they will lift you up in their hands, so that you will not strike your foot against a stone."'
> Jesus answered him, 'It is also written: "Do not put the Lord your God to the test."'
> MATTHEW 4:5–7

To help us think about this part of the story, we're making seed bombs.

You will need: card or paper; peat-free compost; wildflower seeds; water; a bowl; silicone ice cube moulds

Mix up peat-free compost and/or shredded soft cardboard (like egg-boxes, but any card of paper will do) with water to a firm mush. Add wildflower seeds and mix well. Either pack into the ice cube mould and dry in a warm place as quickly as possible (or they'll sprout) to give away and plant later. Or plant them straight away: go up to a high-up window and throw your seed bombs down on to the garden.

Talk about

- The way the seed bomb shatters when it hits the ground and what you think would have happened if Jesus had given in to the temptation to jump.
- The tempter was tempting Jesus to show off and be a selfish superstar miracle-man. How does selfishness damage the planet?
- Should we 'put God to the test' and leave it to God to solve the problems of global warming, pollution and species becoming extinct?
- Which environmental issue is most on your heart?

Part 3

Tell the last part of the story:

> Again, the devil took him to a very high mountain and showed him all the kingdoms of the world and their splendour. 'All this I will give you,' he said, 'if you will bow down and worship me.'
>
> Jesus said to him, 'Away from me, Satan! For it is written: "Worship the Lord your God, and serve him only."'
>
> Then the devil left him, and angels came and attended him.
>
> MATTHEW 4:8–11

To help us think about this part of the story, we're making natural collages.

You will need: paper; glue; as many natural objects as you can find in your garden – leaves, sticks, sand, soil, feathers, seeds, flowers, etc.

As we talk, create a collage out of the items you have.

Talk about

- Whose world is it?
- What responsibility do human beings have for the part they 'own'? What about for the rest of the world, where they don't live?
- What's the most amazing thing (the 'splendour' the tempter refers to) you've ever seen in the world?
- The tempter was inviting Jesus to make a bad bargain. What bad bargains do human beings make that affect the planet?

Part 4: Prayers

Parachute prayers

You will need: string; a small square of cloth; a felt-tip pen; a toy human figure or small weight

Write a prayer for the world on the cloth. Tie each corner to a short piece of string (about 30 cm long) and tie the other ends of the strings to the toy figure or weight. As you throw your parachute from the highest point you can get to safely, pray the prayer you wrote.

Spicy prayers

You will need: a teaspoon of oil; a teaspoon of any smelly spice from the cupboard; an eggcup or small bowl; a cotton bud or stick; paper

Mix your oil and spice together. Think about how far away that spice has come from as you smell it, who grew it, what the climate is like there, what conditions they work in, how far the ship sailed to bring the spice to a shop near you, how interlinked we are around the world. Use the stick and your spice ink to write or draw your prayer for the planet, as you think about these things.

Notes

1 Joel McKerrow, 'As the tamed horse still hears' (Northumbria Community): northumbriacommunity.org/meditations/meditation-day-29. Used by permission.

2 George Lings (ed.), *Messy Church Theology* (BRF, 2013), pp. 156–58 and George Lings, 'Encounters on the Edge No. 46: Messy Church: ideal for all ages?' (Church Army, 2010).

3 Alison Morgan, *The Wild Gospel: Bringing truth to life* (Monarch Books, 2004).

4 Using six different relational routes to aid discipleship piloted and tracked in 'A Voyage of Discovery: Deepening discipleship in Messy Church' (Church Army, 2021).

5 George Lings, *The Day of Small Things: An analysis of fresh expressions of Church in 21 dioceses of the Church of England* (Church Army, 2017), p. 45, with specific figures for Messy Church on p. 102. See also Church of England, *From Anecdote to Evidence: Findings from the Church Growth Research Programme 2011–2013* (The Church Commissioners for England, 2014) and Claire Dalpra and John Vivian, *Who's There?: The church backgrounds of attenders in Anglican fresh expressions of Church* (Church Army's Research Unit, 2016).

6 '65.3% (6,890) of our churches have less than five children or young people under the age of 16 on a Sunday' from General Synod, 'Report from the Evangelism Task Group and the Evangelism and Discipleship Team': churchofengland.org/sites/default/files/2019-01/GS%202118.pdf.

7 Lucy Moore, *All-Age Worship* (BRF, 2010) or see Margaret Withers, *Mission-Shaped Children: Moving towards a child-centred church* (Church House Publishing, 2006).

8 The criteria in the Church of England for assessing whether a person is a pioneer include this attitude.

9 Antoine de Saint-Exupéry, *The Little Prince* (Egmont, 2009), p. 6.

10 Claire Dalpra, *Playfully Serious: How Messy Church create a new space for faith* (Church Army, 2019), see chart p. 9. See also Lings, *The Day Of Small Things*, table p. 183.

11 John Cleese and Robyn Skinner, *Life and How to Survive It* (Ebury Publishing, 1993).

12 worldwildlife.org/press-releases/68-average-decline-in-species-

population-sizes-since-1970-says-new-wwf-report: 68% decline 1970–2016, now estimated at 70%.

13 ghana.arocha.org/projects/protecting-atewa-forest: the forest is under threat from bauxite mining (to make aluminium) but contains amazing and unique wildlife including pangolins and the recently discovered atewa puddle frog which is found nowhere else. A Rocha Ghana is a Christian organisation leading the global campaign to protect Atewa both for people (it is a major source of drinking water) and for wildlife.

14 en.wikipedia.org/wiki/Benedicite#Common_Worship

15 lutheranworld.org/sites/default/files/2019/documents/season_of_creation_2019_resource.pdf, pp. 26–27.

16 Richard Louv, *Last Child in the Woods: Saving our children from nature-deficit disorder* (Algonquin Books, 2005).

17 You can read more about it in *Book of Wonders: Exploring the great mysteries of the universe* (Scripture Union, 2020).

18 You can learn more about how we can forecast the weather from the UK Met Office website: metoffice.gov.uk/weather/learn-about/how-forecasts-are-made.

19 Check out the 'Climate Stripe' for your country at showyourstripes.info: each stripe is a single year, the different colours indicating cooler years (blues) and warmer years (reds). Around the world, in the last 30 to 40 years you can see the climate warming.

20 climate.gov/news-features/understanding-climate/climate-change-atmospheric-carbon-dioxide

21 To find out more about how the climate will change through the 21st century, check out the Met Office climate change website: metoffice.gov.uk/weather/climate-change/what-is-climate-change.

22 bmsworldmission.org/people/laura-lee-lovering

23 Climate Stewards Carbon Calculator: climatestewards.org/carbon-calculators.

24 John Hegley, *Stanley's Stick* (Hodder, 2011).

25 Garry Worete Deverell, *Gondwana Theology: A Trawloolway man reflects on Christian faith* (Morning Star Publishing, 2018), p. 10.

26 The Uniting Church in Australia, 'Revised Preamble to the Constitution': assembly.uca.org.au/images/stories/covenanting/PreamblePoster-web.pdf.

27 Deverell, *Gondwana Theology*, p. 11.

28 YouTube, 'Pee power: Recharge your mobile phone with urine | ABC News', youtube.com/watch?v=buJhuJIACx0.

29 afn.ca/honoring-water

This resource offers Messy Churches the tools to use science to explore aspects of the Christian faith; demonstrate that science and faith are complementary; and enable children and adults alike to appreciate the wonder of creation. 100 sizzling ideas from a range of contributors provide inspiration for the Bible-based activities element of Messy Church.

Messy Church Does Science
100 sizzling science-based ideas for Messy Churches
Edited by David Gregory
978 0 85746 579 5 £9.99

brfonline.org.uk

In this fully revised and expanded new edition, Barry Brand and Pete Maidment offer 80 activities for Messy Church sessions, carefully crafted to appeal to male as well as female participants. They challenge the assumption that Messy Church 'isn't really for men or boys' and offer approaches to engage men and boys in an intentional way. Featuring sections on Big Stuff, Construction, Science, Arty and Edible Crafts, this book provides inspiration for creating a Messy Church that everyone will love to be part of.

Extreme Crafts for Messy Churches
80 activity ideas for the adventurous
Barry Brand and Pete Maidment
978 0 85746 973 1 £9.99

brfonline.org.uk

This collection of perspectives, edited by Messy Church founder Lucy Moore, brings academic analysis and practitioner wisdom to bear on discipleship, a key question for today's church, capturing the latest thinking and learning from the Messy Church context. Individual chapters examine each of the core Messy Church values and how these work in practice to promote discipleship.

Messy Discipleship
Messy Church perspectives on growing faith
Edited by Lucy Moore
978 0 85746 953 3 £8.99

brfonline.org.uk

Holy Habits meets Messy Church! The Holy Habits approach explores Luke's model of church found in Acts 2:42–47, identifies ten habits and encourages the development of a way of life formed by them. This session material has been created to help churches explore the Holy Habits in a Messy Church context and live them out in whole-life, missional discipleship.

Holy Habits in Messy Church
Discipleship sessions for churches
Lucy Moore and Andrew Roberts
978 0 85746 923 6 £8.99

brfonline.org.uk

Seriously Messy

Making space for families to talk together about death and life

Joanna Collicutt, Lucy Moore, Martyn Payne and Victoria Slater

When families experience bereavement and loss, it can be hard for the wider church community to know how best to support them. In this book, four experienced authors and practitioners offer inter-generational approaches for engaging with questions of death and life in a safe and supportive setting. The material guides church communities who are dealing with the death of loved ones and other situations of loss in talking together as a church family, in applying the Christian message of the resurrection in challenging situations, and in listening to each other and developing their own insights.

Seriously Messy
Making space for families to talk together about death and life
Joanna Collicutt, Lucy Moore, Martyn Payne and Victoria Slater
978 0 85746 823 9 £8.99

brfonline.org.uk

Church, but not as you know it

Messy Church is a way of being church for families and others, primarily those who don't already belong to another form of church. It is Christ-centred, for all ages, based on creativity, hospitality and celebration.

Find out more at messychurch.org.uk

brf.org.uk

Enabling all ages to grow in faith

Anna Chaplaincy
Living Faith
Messy Church
Parenting for Faith

100 years of BRF

2022 is BRF's 100th anniversary! Look out for details of our special new centenary resources, a beautiful centenary rose and an online thanksgiving service that we hope you'll attend. This centenary year we're focusing on sharing the story of BRF, the story of the Bible – and we hope you'll share your stories of faith with us too.

Find out more at **brf.org.uk/centenary**.

To find out more about our work, visit
brf.org.uk